W9-AHF-717

The Rights Fight

A Christian Response to America's Debate About Rights

JAY LUCAS

Copyright © 2011 by Jay Lucas

All rights reserved. No part of this book may be used, reproduced, stored in a retrieval system, or transmitted in any form whatsoever — including electronic, photocopy, recording — without prior written permission from the author, except in the case of brief quotations embodied in critical articles or reviews.

Scripture quotations, unless otherwise noted, are taken from the *The ESV® Bible (The Holy Bible, English Standard Version®)* copyright © 2001 by Crossway Bibles, a publishing ministry of Good News Publishers. ESV® Text Edition: 2007.

Additional Scripture quotations are taken from the *Holy Bible, New International Version®*. NIV®. Copyright© 1973, 1978, 1984 by International Bible Society. Used by permission of Zondervan. All rights reserved.

FIRST EDITION

ISBN: 9781936989263

Library of Congress Control Number: 2011939621

Published by
NewBookPublishing.com, a division of Reliance Media, Inc.
2395 Apopka Blvd., #200, Apopka, FL 32703
NewBookPublishing.com

Printed in the United States of America

fact, most people would be shocked to learn that, were it not for God, not only would they have no rights, but there would also be no such thing as rights.

Justifying that controversial claim – that the very existence of rights depends upon God – provides the basis for this book. Discussion and claims about rights are prevalent in America, and it is important for Christians to understand what the Bible teaches about rights. But my interest goes far beyond merely instructing Christians about this one particular element of the Christian worldview, as important as that is.[2] My interest in rights includes both apologetics and evangelism. Apologetics is the branch of theology that offers a defense of Christian truth claims. Apologetics comes from the Greek word *apologia* and refers to a defense such as that which would be offered in a courtroom.

Brothers and fathers, hear the defense
(apologia) that I now make before you.

Acts 22:1

But in your hearts honor Christ the Lord
as holy, always being prepared to make a
defense (apologia) to anyone who asks you
for a reason for the hope that is in you; yet do
it with gentleness and respect.

I Peter 3:15

---

2 A worldview is a person's core beliefs which provide him with a lens through which he sees and interprets the world and his place in it. A worldview will include beliefs about the existence or non-existence of God, the nature of reality, the meaning and purpose of life and a moral code. There is a distinctly Christian worldview, although many Christians have not been taught it.

Evangelism refers to communicating the gospel of Jesus Christ to non-Christians and inviting them to acknowledge Jesus Christ as their Lord and Savior. In many ways, this book is intended to be a training manual for practicing evangelism and apologetics in a culture that obsesses about rights. I believe this method of evangelism can be understood and mastered by almost any Christian who is willing to read and reflect upon this book.

I also hope that non-Christians will read this book, even if it is for the express purpose of refuting it. If you are not a Christian, I hope you will become one.[3] Why would I desire this for you? Because you have a soul that will survive the death of your physical body, and there is a heaven to be gained and a hell to be avoided. In a remarkable way, I believe that the existence of rights is intricately linked to the One who died on the cross for the sins of others. Consider the words of John 1:12:

> But to all who received Him, who believed in His name, **He gave the right** to become children of God.

Of all the rights a person can possess, none could possibly be more important than to be granted the right to be a child of God. This is not a birthright in the sense that a person automatically possesses it by virtue of being born. People are not born as children of God. However, in another sense it is a birthright by virtue of experiencing a second birth, something beautifully described in John 3:3-18. A fuller explanation of the rights that come from a

---

3 I invite you to read Appendix C: *An Open Letter to Non-Christians.*

second birth will be given in Chapter Eleven: "The Right to Eternal Life."[4]

Although I hope many non-Christians will read this book, it is primarily written for Christians. To the Christian reader, I direct this exhortation: Read and master the contents of this book. You must not be content to leave the defense of the Christian view of rights in the hands of pastors, Christian educators, and Christian civil leaders. This should be a matter of concern for all Christians, because it affects all of us.

One of my primary goals in writing this book is to help Christians understand what it means to live in Athens rather than Jerusalem. In using the Athens-Jerusalem comparison, I am drawing upon a situation that existed 2,000 years ago which illustrates where American culture is today. Christianity was born in Jerusalem, a city where almost everyone had a worldview deeply influenced by the Old Testament. When the Christians in Jerusalem shared the gospel with their neighbors, they were dealing with people who already understood much of the Bible. They did not disagree about the existence of God or whether the Scriptures were the Word of God. In that setting the only real question was, "Is Jesus of Nazareth the Messiah?"

With the passing of time, the gospel began to spread to other cities in the Roman Empire. Many of those cities had synagogues where Jews and God-fearing Gentiles

---

4 No claim is being made that we become what Jesus Christ is – the unique and divine Son of God. Being given the right to be God's children changes our standing before God. Other passages add to this concept by talking about the rights of adopted sons and being co-heirs with Christ (see Romans 8:14-17). Nevertheless, Jesus will always be the unique, one of a kind, eternal Son of God.

gathered, and the gospel could be communicated there the same way it had been in Jerusalem. But Christians such as the Apostle Paul eventually took the gospel to people and places where there was no knowledge of the Scriptures and where other gods were worshipped. Athens was such a place.[5] Paul's goal was the same in Athens as it was in Jerusalem: To proclaim the death, resurrection and future return of Jesus Christ. But Paul chose a different starting point when preaching in Athens. He did not begin with Jesus' death on the cross, which would have been foolish or meaningless to the Athenians. Paul started with God as Creator and laid a foundation so that he would have common ground with his hearers. Only when that common ground was in place did Paul mention Jesus (see Acts 17:16-31). Paul was not ashamed of the gospel of Jesus Christ; he simply understood what it meant to be in Athens rather than Jerusalem.

There was a time in history when American culture was closer to the culture of Jerusalem than it was to the culture of Athens. Obviously this is not meant in a racial sense; it refers to worldviews (ideas and beliefs). Two hundred years ago, the vast majority of Americans had some personal knowledge of the Bible. When a child was being taught to read, the Bible was a primary teaching tool. Today, the story is much different. Tens of millions of Americans have had little or no exposure to the contents of the Bible, and our culture is far more

---

5 Athens had a synagogue and he did speak there (see Acts 17:17), but Paul's most important encounter in Athens was with the Greek philosophers he spoke to in the Areopagus (see Acts 17:19).

secular than in the past.[6] In other words, we live in Athens, not Jerusalem. This book will focus on the two major approaches to rights that have influenced America: Christianity and secularism. Human rights are viewed differently in other parts of the world due to the influences of Islam and Eastern philosophy, but *The Rights Fight* is about the debate here in America. Our focus, therefore, will be on Christianity and secularism.

If we are going to be effective in communicating and defending the gospel in our contemporary setting, we first need to establish some common ground with those who are ignorant of or hostile toward the Christian worldview. One of the areas where this common ground can be found is in the mutual concern Americans have about rights. As I stated previously, Americans live in the most rights-conscious culture in history. This passion for rights can be a platform upon which a bridge to the gospel can be built.

I believe the best way to frame the issue of rights is to ask three questions:

1) What is a right?
2) Where do rights come from?
3) How do you know?

Those who reject the Bible and the Christian worldview will stumble over these three questions. I am not saying they won't offer answers. We will be looking at some of the non-biblical answers that have been circulated

---

6 The term "secular," as used here, refers to the absence of a religious or divine element. It is non-religious. Some Christians mistakenly assume that anything which is called secular is to be viewed negatively. "Secular" is a technical term which can be used in a value-neutral way. However, it is true that in Christian writings the word "secular" is frequently employed to convey something which is negative. Although one can be a secularist without being an atheist, in this book the two terms (secular and atheism), will often be used interchangeably.

in recent years. I do believe these non-Christian positions are demonstrably false and that when they are subjected to close inspection, there is something about them that the human heart instinctively knows to be wrong. This doesn't stop some non-Christians from clinging to them, however. As a sample of what we will be encountering, consider these words from famed Professor of Law at Harvard Law School, Alan Dershowitz:

> It is we who create morality, for better or worse, because there is no morality "out there" waiting to be discovered or handed down from some mountaintop. It is because I am a skeptic that I am a moralist. It is because there is no morality beyond human invention that we must devote so much energy to the task of building morality, law and rights. We cannot endure without morality, law and *rights, yet they do not exist unless we bring them into existence.* [7]
>
> (emphasis added)

Dr. Dershowitz has made an amazing statement about rights. He claims that no rights exist outside of human invention. So why is there a right to life according to Dr. Dershowitz? Because someone thought it would be a good idea, and so it was invented. He believes there is no absolute necessity for the right to life, nothing about the nature of the universe or the nature of man that makes it real. Please note that human inventions have a habit

---

7 Alan Dershowitz, *Rights From Wrongs: A Secular Theory of the Origins of Rights* (New York: Basic Books, 2005), p. 79.

of becoming obsolete with the passing of time. There was a time when people marveled at the electric typewriter and business supply stores did a brisk business selling typewriters. Have you seen any typewriter stores lately? Whether he would admit it or not, Dr. Dershowitz's view puts rights in the same category as typewriters. His view of rights and similar views are now dominant in America's most influential law schools. Dr. Dershowitz's view that rights are solely human inventions represents a radical shift away from the American Declaration of Independence (July 4th, 1776):

> We hold these truths to be self-evident: that all men are created equal; that they are endowed, by their Creator, with certain unalienable rights; that among these are life, liberty, and the pursuit of happiness. That to secure these rights, governments are instituted among men ... [8]

Comparing the writings of Dr. Dershowitz to the Declaration of Independence presents a stark contrast. Dr. Dershowitz has also said:

> All theories of natural or *divine rights are legal fictions* created by human beings to satisfy the perceived need for an external

---

8 It is not my intention to critique the strengths and weaknesses of the theology embedded in the Declaration of Independence. For our purposes, let it be noted that America's founding document identifies rights as coming from God, and that one aspect of God's work in creation is that He endows people with rights. Government should secure those rights, but on the most fundamental level, human government and human law are NOT the source of rights. For a theological analysis of the Declaration, I highly recommend Gary Amos' *Defending the Declaration* (Brentwood, Tennessee: Wolgemuth & Hyatt, Publishers, Inc., 1989).

and eternal source of rights to check the wrongs produced by human nature and positive laws.

(emphasis added)

Is Dr. Dershowitz a lone voice when it comes to treating rights as mere human inventions?

Eminent philosopher Alasdair McIntyre has written:

I mean those rights which are alleged to belong to human beings as such and which are cited as a reason for holding that people ought not to be interfered with in their pursuit of life, liberty, and happiness ... the truth is plain: there are no such rights, and belief in them is one with belief in witches and unicorns ... *Natural or human rights then are fictions* ...[9]

(emphasis added)

Not only do I reject Dr. McIntyre's claims that natural or human rights are fictions, but I also believe the actual fiction is that one can reject the biblical worldview yet still construct a meaningful system of rights. William Penn (1644 – 1718) was correct when he said men will be governed by God or they will be ruled by tyrants. The ancients used the term "tyrannos," which meant "he who

9 Alasdair McIntyre, *After Virtue: A Study in Moral Theory.* (South Bend, Indiana: University of Notre Dame Press, 1981), pp 66-67. Dr. McIntyre's comments cited here are not an attack against Christianity, but against the intellectual movement known as the Enlightenment. Unfortunately, I believe that Dr. McIntyre's critique against the Enlightenment has caused some collateral damage.

rules without divine sanction."

Now, about those three questions concerning rights (What is a right? Where do rights come from? How do you know?): How does the Bible answer those questions and why are those answers preferable to non-Christian views? In the following chapters answers will be given to those questions.

Perhaps the most important definition is of the word "right," a term which is central to this book. As a starting point, I would say that a right can be defined as *"a just power to make a moral claim upon someone."*[10] For there to be a just power, it has to derive from something sufficient to account for it. Nothing short of God can account for the existence of a truly just power. The key term here is not "power," but "just." If there are no moral absolutes, then the word "just" will be reduced to moral relativism.

Suppose I were to aim a loaded gun at your head and say to you, "I am going to kill you for the sheer pleasure of the sensation." If you were to ask, "Jay, what gives you the right to kill me?" my response would be, "This gun gives me the right." Do you see what has happened here? The gun gives me the *power* to kill you, but it is not a *just* power. For me to use the power of the gun in this instance

---

10 This definition of a right comes from J. Budziszewski, *What We Can't Not Know* (Dallas: Spence Publishing Company, 2003), p. 23. There are various definitions of a right used by legal scholars and philosophers, but most of them will make common use of concepts such as duties, protections, privileges, and immunities that people have as individuals or groups. Interestingly, many books and articles that address the issue of rights do not even define what is meant by a "right." There is an assumption that most people know what the term means. The conflict is usually about the extent of rights (what counts as a right and who possesses that right?) and the source of rights (where do they come from?). I think it is a mistake to skip the most basic question, "What is a right?" For reasons I will make clear, I think Dr. Budziszewski's definition is outstanding.

would be unjust. My claim upon your life would not be a moral claim. In other words, I do not have the right to kill you even though I have the power to kill you. In this example, you are the one who possesses a right, not me. You have the right (the just power) to make a moral claim upon me. That is, you have the right to make a moral claim upon me if, and only if, the biblical worldview is true. Deny the biblical worldview and you will surrender the necessary foundation for judging my use of power against you to be unjust. The inseparable link between morality and rights will be made manifest in the following chapters.

This is a good time to explain the difference between objective and subjective rights. When I speak of rights as being objective, I mean that the basis of their existence is external to man because they reflect the moral will of God and they manifest His thoughts. "It is wrong to murder" is an objective moral absolute that can be restated as "It is right not to murder." The focus is on the moral standard which is external to any particular individual. Subjective rights put the emphasis on the rights-holder, as in, "I have the right not to be murdered." Because "It is right not to murder" (an objective standard external to any particular individual), I have the right not to be murdered (a subjective right). These terms and concepts will become clearer as we progress through this book.

Remember, we are interested in three questions:
1) What is a right?
2) Where do rights come from?
3) How do you know?

We have given a preliminary answer to the first question by saying that a right is the just power to make a moral claim upon someone. Question two asks about the origin of rights (Where do rights come from?). At the most basic level, we can recognize that rights either come from God (as taught in the Bible and recognized by the Declaration of Independence), or they do not come from God (as asserted by Dr. Dershowitz). If we were to ask Dr. Dershowitz the third question (How do you know?), he would say that he knows rights do not come from God because God does not exist.

There is no shortage of people who gladly join Dr. Dershowitz in denying that rights depend upon God. I believe the fundamental reason for this denial about the divine origin of rights is rooted in the desire to deny God Himself. If a right is the just power to make a moral claim upon someone and if God is the source of rights, then the unavoidable implication is that we are morally accountable to God. If you do not like the prospect of being morally accountable to God, then you need to devise a theory of rights that excludes God. American legal philosophy has been attempting to accomplish that for more than a century, and it is a recipe for disaster.

As I have stated, this book is about both apologetics and evangelism. It is an apologetic (a reasoned defense) for the biblical view of the divine origin of rights.[11] Regardless of what is being taught in some law schools today, the

---

11 This book is not intended to be a text about the technical details of rights theories. That would require an entirely separate volume. This book is about the foundation of rights and my claim that the only reliable foundation for rights is the Christian God. A brief description of the various aspects of rights is provided in Chapter Nine: "Getting Rights Right."

truth of the matter is that objective human rights exist as a result of how God has created and ordered the universe. For a right to be valid, it must have objective existence in the sense that God's moral standards are reflected in whatever justification is given for that right. The right to exterminate people in gas chambers might exist in a particular human law code, but such a right does not truly exist in God's universe.

Not all rights claims are valid, but any rights claim that is consistent with the biblical worldview is valid; such rights do exist. Rights are a reflection of God's justice, His moral standards, and the duties He imposes on the moral agents He has created. Justice is a norm imposed by God and required of men in their relationships with each other. The justice God requires of one person implies the existence of a right on behalf of the person to whom that justice is due.[12] This is why I use the definition of a right as being *a just power to make a moral claim upon someone.* I offer this apologetic for five reasons:

1) A passion for God's glory and the desire to see His authority proclaimed and understood.

2) A burden to see Christians equipped to share the gospel effectively in a rights-intoxicated culture.

3) A desire to see Christians strengthened in their faith.

4) A love for my children and the desire to see them live in a society safeguarded from secular and religious tyranny.

---

12 It is not necessarily true that every duty implies a right. Our focus will be on those duties that do imply corresponding rights.

5) A love for my neighbors (see Luke 10:25-37 for Jesus' parable of the Good Samaritan) and a desire to see them live in a society safeguarded from secular and religious tyranny.

The Rights Fight is not an explicit call to political activism and it offers no political strategy. As I have stated, this book is about apologetics and evangelism. My desire is to use this discussion about rights as a platform from which to proclaim the gospel of Jesus Christ, about whom it is written:

He was in the world,
and the world was made through Him,
yet the world did not know Him.
He came to His own,
and His own people did not receive Him.
But to all who did receive Him,
who believed in His name,
HE GAVE THE RIGHT
to become children of God.
(John 1:10-12)

This wonderful news should be at the center of a Christian response to America's debate about rights.

Chapter Two:

Speaking Of Rights

There are three possible ways to understand the nature of rights:

1) Rights do not exist.
2) Rights exist only because they are created by human law.
3) Rights exist because they are created by God.

The purpose of this book is to explain and defend the third option, the one that says rights exist because they are created by God. The proposition that rights exist because they are created by God lends itself to the proclamation of the gospel of Jesus Christ. The individual who, by faith, acknowledges Jesus Christ as Lord and Savior becomes a legal heir to eternal blessings, a right which God gives to His children (see Romans 8:17). In defending this proposition it will be necessary to critique the first two options and explain why they are untrue, why they are irrational, and why they ultimately lead to tyranny.[13] The thoughtful Christian is not only interested in how rights have a place in the doctrine of eternal life, but he is also interested in how rights should function in the interaction between individuals and in the relationship between the citizen and the state. Throughout this book, repeated references will be made to universal objective human rights. What does that include? For the sake of clarity we will limit it to:

1) A basic right to life.
2) The right to worship God according to the dictates of conscience, both individually and in gatherings of like-minded believers.
3) The right to own property.

I believe these rights are universal (possessed by everyone) and objective (exist apart from any particular individual because their source is external to man). Because *The Rights Fight* is not a textbook on rights, in-depth discussion about all the possible categories of rights will be minimal. Our emphasis will be on the proposition that God is the source of basic human rights and that the gospel of Jesus Christ can be communicated using the concept of rights.

The following dialog is intended to serve as a starting point in the conversation about rights. It will

---

13 There are some rights which can be created by human law. We call these "legal rights." If I possess a legal driver's license and my car is registered and insured, I have the legal right to drive 65 miles per hour on the interstate. This is in keeping with human legislation. Technically speaking, such a right is not found in the Bible nor is there any timeless principle in the Bible which is contradicted by this man-made right. These kinds of legal rights make civilization possible and they are important. However, the focus of this book is of a higher order, namely, universal human rights that are divine in origin. Legal rights will be discussed in Chapter Nine: "Getting Rights Right."

introduce the Christian view of rights that will be developed throughout this book. Our two conversationalists are Kirsten (Christian) and Michelle (non-Christian). They are talking about abortion rights, but the crux of the conversation is not so much about abortion as it is about the foundation of rights in general.[14]

Michelle: The Supreme Court got it right with Roe vs. Wade. How could anyone really justify telling a woman what she can do with her   own body? It is a matter of privacy and it is a constitutional right.

Kirsten: What about the rights of the baby?

Michelle: C'mon, Kirsten. That's a tired argument that doesn't work. A baby living outside the womb is one thing, but a partially developed fetus with no self-awareness can't be considered a possessor of rights.

Kirsten: According to whom?

Michelle: According to the law and to the courts.

Kirsten: Okay, let me ask you this. If the pro-life movement was able to affect the law through legislation, and if they stacked the courts with judges who would uphold the new laws, would you no longer have   the right to an abortion?

Michelle: Thankfully, that's not going to happen. The

---

14 An audible conversation differs in style from a written portrayal of a conversation such as the one which appears here. I chose to focus on the content rather than to replicate the flow of words that sound natural when spoken. While I hope the written conversation seems at least somewhat natural, the emphasis is on content and not style.

days of back alley abortions and coat hangers are behind us.

Kirsten: True or false: Before Roe vs. Wade a woman did not have the right to an abortion.[15]

Michelle: That's a dishonest question and you know it.

Kirsten: Wait a minute, Michelle. You have to decide what your foundation for rights is. Just a moment ago you were appealing to the law and the rulings of our courts as the source of rights. But as you know, prior to 1973, the law in most states and the courts opposed your position. If you had been pregnant in 1953, would you have had a right to an abortion?

Michelle: The right was always there, it just took a long time for it to be recognized. That's not the first time that has happened in history. The issue of slavery is a classic example of this. Changing the law was a way of giving recognition to something that should always have been so.

Kirsten: Michelle, I am still trying to understand what your foundation is. I would like to ask you three basic questions about rights. And, by the way, I want you to feel free to ask me the same questions, and tear my answers apart if you would like. Is that okay?

Michelle: I'm not sure if this will be anything other than a waste of time, but go ahead.

Kirsten: Thanks, Michelle. Now, here are the three

---

15 Before Roe vs. Wade, individual states did have abortion laws, some of which permitted abortion for medical reasons. However, Roe vs. Wade not only swept aside the laws of individual states, it opened the door for abortion on demand, far exceeding what had previously been permitted by law.

questions. What is a right, where do rights come from and how do you know?

Michelle: You can't be serious. It would take an encyclopedia to answer all that.

Kirsten: I know those questions can lead to complex discussions. But I'm not asking you for that. On just the most elementary or basic level, tell me what a right actually is, where it comes from and how you know.

Michelle: I have a right to privacy. A right is a recognition of how someone is entitled to be treated or, to put it a bit differently, to be free from interference by someone else. In the case of a woman's right to choose, she should not be subjected to the interference of someone else telling her what she can or cannot do with her own body.

Kirsten: Whether or not that particular right exists, I agree with you that some rights do exist. But from where do rights come from and how do you know?

Michelle: Abortion is legal. The United States Supreme Court recognized the choice of abortion as a right.

Kirsten: Did they recognize the right, or did they invent it?

Michelle: What do you mean?

Kirsten: Michelle, what I'm trying to uncover is what reason you have for believing you have rights. It seems to me that if rights are something invented and provided by the State, then the

State can also change them or take them away. Under this view, there are no inherent rights that belong to us on the very basis of being human. They are not God-given; they are man-made. Look at it this way: What if our courts and legislatures came under the control of people who said that men can legally rape women who appear in public wearing blue jeans? Men would be given that right and be protected by the State.

Michelle: That's ridiculous.

Kristen: Why?

Michelle: Because no sane person thinks like that.

Kirsten: Don't be so sure of that. But back to my question. If society changed to the point where laws could be passed allowing men to rape women, and if a court upheld the law as being a legal right, would it therefore be okay?

Michelle: Under that scenario, I would say that calling something a legal right doesn't mean someone truly has that right.

Kirsten: I agree 100 percent. A good law may recognize or protect a genuine right, but the most basic human rights don't come from legislation. If rights are something we conjure up, either as individuals or as a society, then they don't really have any objective existence. Why should China feel any obligation to Western concepts of human rights? Are they truly violating rights in Tibet, or when they force   a woman to abort her second child? Who are we to say that they should abide by our sensibilities when it comes to rights? And if a man has a strong desire to rape a woman and the act would bring him pleasure, why can't he claim it as a right?

Michelle: Because granting him that right would be an injustice against his victim. A right that creates an injustice is not a true right.

Kirsten: How do you know that? What is the absolute standard you have which allows you to make that kind of judgment? If you have an absolute standard for what is just or unjust, from where does it come and how do you know?

Michelle: What's yours? Before you continue with giving me the third degree, let me hear your answers. What is a right? Where do rights come from? How do you know?

Kirsten: Fair enough. I'm not close to being an expert in all this, but a basic definition is that a right is a just power to make a moral claim upon someone. For there to be a just power, it has to derive from something sufficient to account for it. Nothing short of God can justify the existence of a truly just power. The key term here is not "power," but "just." And when we talk about something being just, we're going to have to deal with moral absolutes or the word "just" will be reduced to moral relativism. In that case, rights are just a façade that puts a pretty face on the agenda of the most powerful.

The Christian worldview gives us knowledge of God and His absolute moral standards, and He alone can provide the foundation for objective human rights.

Michelle: You've given this some thought; I'll give you credit for that. But you haven't proved your case to me. Why should I accept your answers instead of someone else's?

Kirsten: Suggest an alternative foundation for human rights and we'll critique it together. Michelle, I think you will find that any secular foundation will ultimately reduce to moral relativism and that leads to tyranny. I know that people give it clean labels like "enlightened self-interest," but the bottom line is it will be arbitrary, and that means your so-called rights can be arbitrarily taken away from you.

~ ~ ~ ~ ~

We will break into the conversation at this point. Michelle instinctively knows that a man does not have the right to rape a woman, no matter how emphatically he claims to have it. That right does not exist, and any law which supposedly creates that right is absurd and unjust. At the same time, Michelle is certain that she has a right to an abortion, and even without the force of pro-abortion laws, she would still believe such a right exists. Kirsten was simultaneously asking questions and laying the groundwork for a biblical view of rights.

Kirsten identified a serious inconsistency in

Michelle's defense of abortion rights. Actually, to call it an inconsistency is generous; it is really a contradiction. If Michelle wants to appeal to the authority of human law as being a sufficient basis for abortion rights, then what grounds would she have for rejecting the sufficiency of human law if a law were passed which legalized rape? Later in this book, we will see how it is both possible and practical to take this kind of conversation as a platform for presenting the gospel.

Michelle's view of rights and law are an outgrowth of what is called legal positivism, and it is the philosophy of law that dominates the classroom discussions in many American law schools. The last several generations of lawyers, judges and legislators have been taught legal positivism[16]. At its core, legal positivism is the rejection of any transcendent, metaphysical or supernatural foundations for law.[17] In other words, there is no "higher law." The entire realm of law is limited to whatever laws men create. J. Daryl Charles makes this observation:

> Because there is no authority beyond human
> experience and outside of human willpower

---

16 Fortunately, not everyone who has been taught legal positivism accepts it as true.

17 The term "transcendent" means to be above or beyond a particular order, realm or sphere. To say, "Tiger Woods transcends the sport of golf" is to say that his fame is not limited to golf fans. Millions of people who have no interest in golf have an interest in Tiger Woods. To say, "God is transcendent" is to say that God exists beyond or outside the created realm of nature. To say that there is a transcendent law or there are transcendent rights is to look beyond or outside of the temporal realm of the laws or rules that people make. The term "metaphysical" refers to a reality beyond or behind a particular physical instance of a thing. Is the human mind completely reducible to the electro-chemical reactions occurring in the brain, or does the mind include a reality beyond physical processes of the brain? This is a metaphysical question.

that informs and guides human morality, human "rights" are subjectively identified and culturally based, since there is no universally determinate "human nature."

The implication, though not explicit among positivists, is that human rights cannot exist where society does not acknowledge them.[18]

One of the primary intellectual roots of legal positivism is naturalistic evolution or, as it is also known, "Darwinism." When Charles Darwin published his *Origin of Species* in 1859, he energized a revolution of ideas that went far beyond biology. Since man was the product of natural (no supernatural) processes working over eons of time, many of man's activities could also be reduced to evolutionary processes. The academic disciplines of religion, economics, history, psychology, sociology, political science and law were now imbided with a Darwinian interpretation.[19] If God is no longer needed to explain what we see in nature, why do we need Him to explain law, morality or human rights?

---

18   J. Daryl Charles, *Retrieving the Natural Law: A Return to Moral First Things* (Grand Rapids, Michigan: Eerdmans Publishing, 2008), p. 17.

19 French philosopher Auguste Comte (1798-1857) was the founder of positivism. Initially, positivism was applied to science and it asserted that sense experience and the natural sciences are the source of all human knowledge. Theological and metaphysical concerns were swept aside and relegated to the trash heap of primitive superstition and obsolete human history. Darwin's *Origin of Species* came at the perfect time to ride the momentum begun by Comte and others. When Comte's positivism and Darwin's natural selection were applied to law, the result was legal positivism. Supreme Court Chief Justice Oliver Wendell Holmes (1841 – 1935) was one of the early proponents of legal positivism.

In his analysis of legal positivism, John Eidsmoe identifies these six central tenets:

1) A denial of divine absolutes. Even if there are God-given standards of law, they are completely irrelevant in our contemporary legal system.

2) Law is what the lawmaker (man) says it is, and nothing more. The State is the author of law.

3) Law is constantly changing and evolving. Just as man is evolving and changing, so must law. Nothing is permanent.

4) Law is judge-made. Their rulings determine how law will evolve.

5) Law is learned by studying cases. There is no divine original law from which we learn.

6) There are no God-given human rights. The State creates rights through the law.[20]

Legal positivism does, in a limited way, make some valid points about how law can function. The problem is that it is like a beautiful house lovingly built upon a foundation of sand. The builders and onlookers admire the house, for it is very appealing to the eye. As long as the weather remains mild everything seems fine. But just beneath the surface there is a disaster waiting to happen. When a severe enough storm presses against the house, the folly of building upon a foundation of sand will become tragically evident, and the good intentions of the builders will mean very little to the occupants

---

20 John Eidsmoe, *The Christian Legal Advisor,* (Milford, Michigan: Mott Media, 1984), pp. 75-84.

trapped inside the collapsed house.

On the surface, legal positivism is a rational system. Or, to put it another way, legal positivism reflects the logical implications of what is required to govern a society without God. However, a more thorough analysis will reveal that this system is little more than "might makes right." This explains why contemporary battles over various rights claims in America are always reduced to political might. Ultimately, there is no other consideration that matters. Whoever can gain the upper hand in the political process (and this includes the politicization of the judiciary), will be the arbiter of what rights exist and of who possesses them. The conversation between Kirsten and Michelle hinted at that reality.

Kirsten's questions and comments to Michelle made reference to the concepts of just power, moral relativism, moral absolutes and objective human rights. These concepts will be explained in the following chapters. The Christian worldview recognizes the link that joins morality, law, rights and God. If God is taken out of the equation and replaced with human autonomy, then the nature of morality, law and rights must be radically changed.[21] And that is precisely what has happened in America. People who actually believe that *all men are created equal and are endowed by their Creator with certain unalienable rights, and that among these are life, liberty and the pursuit of happiness* are discovering that they are not

---

21 The term "human autonomy" is based upon the word "auto," which means "self" and "nomos," which means "law." "Autonomy" means self-law or self-rule. "Human autonomy" means that man is a law or rule unto himself and God is excluded.

welcome in current policy debates about rights. Although the conversation between Kirsten and Michelle was fairly brief, my intention for Michelle is that she be seen as the portrayal of countless millions of Americans. We love our rights, we believe they are very meaningful and we howl in protest if someone seeks to infringe upon them or refuses to acknowledge their existence. As passionate as we are about rights, most of us have never asked ourselves, or asked others, these three basic questions:

1) What is a right?
2) Where do rights come from?
3) How do you know?

Any system or philosophy of law that attempts to answer these questions while excluding God and the biblical worldview will be like the emperor in Hans Christian Andersen's story, *The Emperor's New Suit* (1837). This emperor was very vain. One day, two swindlers tell the emperor that they have made a new suit for him out of a special material that is invisible to anyone who is unfit for office and to those who are exceptionally stupid. Although the emperor cannot see the suit, he is not about to admit it for fear of being considered unfit or stupid. For the same reasons, no one around the emperor will admit that they also cannot see the suit. Finally, while the emperor is "wearing" the new suit in public, a young boy speaks out about the emperor's suit by making the truthful observation that the emperor is not wearing any clothes at all, that, in fact, he is naked! This is an amusing story, which also paints an accurate portrait of those who believe they can construct a just system of laws and rights while excluding God.

> *There is a way that seems right to a man,*
> *but its end is the way to death.*
>
> Proverbs 14:12

Chapter Three:

The Stakes Are High

When it comes to beliefs about rights, people can be divided into two basic groups. There are those who believe that rights come from God and depend upon Him, and there are those who believe that rights do *not* come from God and do *not* depend upon Him. Certainly, there are sub-categories within this basic twofold grouping, but for our present purposes we will concern ourselves with these two groups. The stakes are incalculably high for both groups. In fact, the stakes are so high that we must be on guard against the possibility of dishonest, inconsistent or self-deceiving argumentation from apologists on both sides.

What is at stake for the pro-God side?[22] Since I am a member of this group, I will speak in terms of what is at stake for me. If I am wrong about rights then I am

---

22 Remember, I am using this term as a reference to a distinctively biblical and Christian worldview.

guilty of misrepresenting the teachings of the Bible. This might not seem like a big deal to a non-Christian, but for someone who believes that the Bible is the Word of God, to be guilty of misrepresenting it, even unintentionally, is a matter of great concern. James 3:1 says,

> *Not many of you should become teachers, my brothers, for you know that we who teach will be judged with greater strictness.*

My concern at this point is not whether the Bible is true. Assuming, for the moment, that the Bible is true (in the sense that it is the Word of God), what does it teach about rights? If I am imposing a modern Western theory of rights upon the Bible in a way that is contrary to what the Bible actually teaches, then I am guilty of committing a very serious error against God's Word.

As I reflect further on my personal stake in this debate, my concern grows deeper. What if I am able to construct a philosophy of rights that is consistent with the Bible, but the Bible itself is not true? What if the Bible is not the Word of God?[23] My concern here is not that I have chosen the wrong side in a public policy debate; rather, my concern is that my entire life's purpose and my entire belief system are bankrupt. And at this level I am not thinking merely about my present life in this physical body in this temporal world. The belief system that provides

---

23   The issue of the Bible's divine inspiration, infallibility and truthfulness is directly linked to my position on rights. This book is not intended to provide an exhaustive and highly technical argument for the Bible. There are many scholarly and competent works available which provide a defense of the Bible. Nevertheless, I will give a basic apology in Chapter Six, which is to be expected if I am serious about answering the third question about rights, "How do you know?"

the foundation for my view of rights goes far beyond any debate about rights. It goes to the most serious question of all: "What happens to me when I die?"

The third major concern I have when I consider what is at stake in the rights fight is the safety and freedom (both religious and political) of my children and perhaps, someday, my grandchildren. Fyodor Dostoyevsky (1821-1881) famously said that if there is no immortality, then all things are permissible. We can state that in a slightly different way: "If there are no objective divine human rights, then all things are permissible." I am not going to use a voice of moderation in explaining this, because without the existence of objective human rights there is no true obligation for someone to exercise moral restraint. I refuse to give the legal positivist a pass on this.

Let me state this as plainly as possible. If there are no objective moral values, then there are no objective human rights.[24]   As I noted in my introduction to this book, Harvard Law School Professor Alan Dershowitz states that it is we who create morality, law and rights. They have no objective existence outside of us and we do not discover them. They are inventions; we bring them into existence. As we will see, this position is thinly veiled tyranny while also being one step removed from anarchy.

In   Chapter   Eight: "Secular   Dreams   and Nightmares," I will explain the link between objective moral values and objective human rights. In anticipation of that discussion, I will make this claim: If there are no

---

24   The word "objective," as used here, speaks of that which has existence or standing outside of individual human experience.   An objective moral value is a value that is absolute and universal. It is not relative to any particular individual, and thus, it is the opposite of moral relativism and subjective individualism.

objective moral values and no objective human rights, then there is nothing truly immoral about the torture, rape and murder of a young child. Under such conditions, no deed, no matter how heinous or unjust it might seem to be, could ever be shown to be wrong in an absolute sense. Society might punish the deed, but that would not make the deed wrong. Society might say that it has passed laws giving a child the right not to be molested, but why could not society have just as easily passed a law that gives molesters the right to rape children? What if two adjoining countries passed contrary laws (with legal rights embedded in those laws), and one country sided with children and the other society sided with molesters? Are both sets of rights equally valid? If there are no objective moral values (values rooted in God, not the invention of man) and no objective human rights (rights endowed by the Creator), then there is no more justice in punishing the molester than there is in protecting the molester. It would simply be a matter of man-made law.

I have been honest about what is at stake for me. My faith in the truthfulness of the Christian worldview not only determines my values and priorities for this present life, but also gives me hope of a life after death. I trust the biblical promise of John 1:12, that by believing in the Lord Jesus Christ I have been given *the right* to become a child of God.

Perhaps the nature of my personal investment in the rights fight means that I am willing to accept a position which is irrational. Don't get me wrong; I am very committed to rationality. Nevertheless, I understand why a skeptic would be suspicious of both my reasoning processes and my faith commitments. But what about the flip side of the coin? What about the reasoning processes and the faith commitments of the person who denies a divine, supernatural or theistic foundation for rights? Are not the stakes just as high for him? Do I not have a right (no pun intended!) to be suspicious of his potential irrationality? What is at stake for the person who rejects the Christian worldview?

When someone denies that God is the source of rights, he is making a wager with his soul.[25] He is denying that there is a just and righteous God who will judge people for their violation of His moral standards. This is a losing bet because not only is God the source of whatever human rights do exist, but God is also the universe's ultimate rights-holder. God has rights that sinful humanity constantly violates. God has a right to be worshiped and obeyed on His exclusive terms (the first two of the Ten Commandments in Exodus 20:3-6). God has a right to impose moral standards on the creatures He has made. The Potter (God) has the right to rule over the clay (man):

> *Has the potter no right over the clay, to make*
> *out of the same lump one vessel for honorable*
> *use and another for dishonorable use?*
> Romans 9:21

Perhaps most importantly, God has a right to judge and to dispense justice:

---

25   This is a reference to objective universal human rights such as the right to life, not the legal rights that vary from society to society.

...because He has fixed a day on which He will judge the world in righteousness by a man whom He has appointed; and of this He has given assurance to all by raising Him from the dead.

Acts 17:31

To be morally accountable to a holy and just God is a disturbing prospect because no one can, on his or her own, stand innocent before that God. We are all law breakers and criminals in God's universe:

Now we know that whatever the law says it speaks to those who are under the law, so that every mouth may be stopped, and the whole world may be held accountable to God ... for all have sinned and fall short of the glory of God ...

Romans 3:19, 23

I began this chapter by acknowledging the serious nature of my personal stake in the rights fight. For me, the ramifications of my position could ripple far beyond this present life because it is related to the question, "What happens to me when I die?" I answer the question of life after death by believing and trusting in God's promises regarding Jesus Christ, the forgiveness of sin, and *the right* to become a child of God. My belief is not just in any god, but in the God who reveals Himself to us through the Bible, meaning the Christian God, the God of Abraham, Isaac and Jacob. It is because of the very nature of God that rights exist. This implies that any theory of rights which denies the divine origin of rights is also a denial of personal accountability to God. Therefore, it is not just the Christian position that has eternal consequences; non-Christian theories of rights also look beyond the grave. Indeed, the stakes are tremendously high for everyone.

I want to press this point home in the most direct terms possible. Based on the biblical worldview, I would respond to the person who denies that God is the source of rights by saying, "You don't really believe what you are professing. Deep down inside, you know that rights depend on God, but you are trying very hard to suppress what you know to be true. There are no genuine legal positivists, only people who outwardly claim to believe something their conscience tells them isn't so." [26]

For the general reader who has not encountered this viewpoint before, such an assertion might be startling. For the legal positivist, it might be infuriating. But this is what the Apostle Paul would say about legal positivists if he were here today, because this is consistent with what Paul wrote in his epistle to the Romans (circa 58 A.D.):

> *For the wrath of God is revealed from heaven*
> *against all ungodliness and unrighteousness*
> *of men, who by their unrighteousness*
> *suppress the truth. For what can be known*

---

26 In this sentence, I am using the concept of legal positivism as a synonym for any theory of law and rights that excludes God in favor of a secular foundation. Not everyone who denies a "higher law" in favor of human autonomy is a legal positivist. Dr. Dershowitz explicitly denies being a legal positivist (*Rights From Wrongs*, pp. 5-8). I am using legal positivism as a representative for all secular theories. I believe my critique of legal positivists in this present chapter is equally true of all non-Christians. Also, not everyone who accepts secular theories of law simultaneously reject belief in God. It is possible to believe in God while embracing legal positivism, but it is also inconsistent and irrational to do so.

about God is plain to them, because God has shown it to them. For His invisible attributes, namely, His eternal power and divine nature, have been clearly perceived, ever since the creation of the world, in the things that have been made.

So they are without excuse. For although they knew God, they did not honor Him as God or give thanks to Him, but they became futile in their thinking, and their foolish hearts were darkened.

Romans 1:18-21

In these verses, Paul made it clear that there is knowledge of God which is possessed by everyone. It is plain to them (verse 19). Because of man's sinful nature, he will choose to suppress the truth that he knows. We must be careful not to say more than Paul said, but we should not accept less than what Paul said, either. Paul did not claim that people naturally possess knowledge of God's redemptive plan of salvation through Jesus Christ. That requires special revelation carried by human messengers to other people.[27] But they at least know that God exists, and they know of His eternal power and divine nature. This knowledge, sparse as it is, is still enough to

---

27   The terms "special revelation" and "general revelation" are very important in our discussion of rights. General revelation refers to knowledge of God that has been available to all people throughout human history. This revelation primarily comes through God's creation of the world, the human moral conscience and God's providential care (see Acts 14:15-17). "Special revelation" refers to information given by God to some people through prophecy, miracles, Scripture and, ultimately, through the incarnation of Jesus Christ.

leave people without excuse (verse 20).[28]

How do we get from the minimal general revelation of Romans 1:18-21 to my claim that there are no legal positivists? I can well imagine that any legal positivist reading this is probably outraged and offended by my claim. After all, I am claiming to know him better than he knows himself, at least as far as his beliefs about rights are concerned. It is not my desire to offend anyone, and I certainly do not intend for my words to be interpreted as being a personal attack. I am simply taking the biblical worldview and using it to assess the claims made on behalf of legal positivism. God is the One who knows us better than we know ourselves and He has given each of us some knowledge of Him.

The knowledge of God that we possess through general revelation is not limited to Romans 1:18-21. In the succeeding verses, Paul discusses various human behaviors that are sinful because they violate God's moral law. Paul then states:

> *Though they know God's decree that those who practice such things deserve to die, they not only do them but give approval to those who practice them.*
>
> Romans 1:32

The interesting thing about verse 32 is that Paul is talking about humanity in general, not those who had received the special revelation of biblical law. Something

---

28   "Without excuse" is a translation of the Greek "anapologetous," which can also be translated as "without apology." In other words, there is no apologetic/defense/apologia for the unbelief of Romans 1:18-21.

about how God has made us enables us to know there are actions that are immoral because they are sins against a holy God, and we can know this without ever having been exposed to the Bible. How do we have this moral knowledge? Paul explains:

> For when Gentiles, who do not have the law, by nature do what the law requires, they are a law to themselves, even though they do not have the law. **They show that the work of the law is written on their hearts,** while their conscience also bears witness, and their conflicting thoughts accuse or even excuse them.
>
> Romans 2:14-15
>
> (emphasis added)

Although I have not yet explained it, I have already submitted the proposition that the Christian worldview teaches that there is a direct link among morality, law, rights and God. In Romans 2:14-15, Paul stated that God gives a moral conscience to all people. Despite all of our diversity and despite our sinful propensity to numb or silence our consciences or to twist what our consciences are telling us about our sin, there are objective moral standards known by all. The existence of rights is rooted in these moral standards, which are revealed by God and written on the heart.

According to the Bible, the human conscience is not the source of moral standards. In his commentary on Romans, Douglas Moo writes:

The conscience is not itself the source of moral norms but functions as a reflective mechanism by which people can measure their conformity to a norm.[29]

God's own righteousness (His moral character) is the source and standard for ethical norms. Those standards are objective in the sense that they originate and have standing outside of and apart from any individual human experiencing them. In keeping with being created in God's image, man has received from God an internal awareness of God's righteous standards (the law God has written on man's heart) and a moral conscience which alerts man to his success or failure to conform to God's standards. The human heart is the tablet upon which morality is written, but God Himself does the writing. This is not to say that God directly speaks to the conscience in the way a human parent audibly speaks to his or her child. But the standards to which the conscience responds come from God, and the operation of the conscience is from God and is a result of God's creative design and purposes for humanity.

There are also subjective influences that are part of the experience of each individual. The presence of subjective factors account for the variables we encounter when comparing different cultures and their differing moral codes with each other (and their differing views of human rights). Are there differences between cultures?

29   Douglas Moo, *The Wycliffe Exegetical Commentary,* Romans 1-8, Kenneth Barker, General Editor (Chicago: Moody Press, 1991), p. 148.

Yes. Are there similarities that more than outweigh those differences? Absolutely yes.

The great Christian scholar C.S. Lewis (1898 - 1963), who had at one time been a convinced atheist, was deeply influenced by what Paul wrote. In his classic, *Mere Christianity*, Lewis observed:

> There have been differences between their moralities, but these have never amounted to anything like a total difference. If anyone will take the trouble to compare the moral teaching of, say, the ancient Egyptians, Babylonians, Hindus, Chinese, Greeks and Romans, what will really strike him will be how very like they are to each other and to our own. I need only ask the reader to think what a totally different morality would mean. Think of a country where people were admired for running away in battle, or where a man felt proud of double-crossing all the people who had been kindest to him. You might just as well try to imagine a country where two and two made five. Men have differed as regards what people you ought to be unselfish to - whether it was only your own family, or your fellow countrymen, or everyone. But they have always agreed that you ought not put yourself first. Selfishness has never been admired. Men have differed as to whether you should have one wife or four. But they have always agreed that

you must not simply have any woman you liked.[30]

If rights are connected to God's moral standards, and if those moral standards are written on everyone's heart, then legal positivism is actually an attempt to suppress what the positivist knows about God and about his accountability to God. Lewis also wrote:

> These, then, are the two points I wanted to make. First, that human beings all over the earth have this curious idea that they ought to behave in a certain way, and cannot really get rid of it. Secondly, that they do not in fact behave that way. They know the Law of Nature; they break it. These two facts are the foundation of all clear thinking about ourselves and the universe we live in.
>
> *Mere Christianity*, p. 7

So you see, the stakes in the rights fight are high for everyone. The rights fight has implications that go far beyond the political and social battles of contemporary American culture. Because of the human desire to neutralize or desensitize a sense of guilt and accountability before a holy God, legal positivism is a philosophy of law and rights that exiles the Divine Lawgiver. The God who is the Author of our duties and our rights is treated as a non-factor. Ironically, in seeking to be free, man has

---

30   C.S. Lewis, *Mere Christianity* (Westwood, New Jersey: Barbour and Company), p. 5. This is a reprint in The Christian Library series with permission from Macmillan Publishing Company.

chosen a legal philosophy that erodes the foundation for freedom (political and spiritual) and has placed us on the road to tyranny.

Chapter Four:

And God Said, "Let There Be Rights"

If the title of this chapter was, "And God Said, Let There be Light," would you know where to find that in the Bible? Most Christians would immediately recognize those words as being among the first verses of the Bible. The creation account is found in Genesis 1, and the third verse records this decree: "And God said, 'Let there be light,' and there was light." Even many non-Christians could identify the location of those words in the Bible. But where in the Bible do you find this verse: "Then God said, 'Let there be rights,' and there were rights"? No such verse with those particular words exists, but the first seeds of human rights are found in Genesis 1, and the rest of the Bible cultivates those seeds.

The Bible was not specifically written to serve as a treatise on human rights. It should also be noted that for many centuries into the Christian era there was little or no discussion of human rights among Christian theologians, at least not as we perceive human rights.[31] There were many historical reasons for this, but it is certainly the case that the foundational truths or seeds needed for objective human rights are found in Scripture.

This chapter will provide an answer to the second of our three questions about rights. The first question, "What is a right?" has been given this initial answer: A right is the just power to make a moral claim upon someone. Although there is more we will say about that first question and answer, we will now consider the second question, "Where do rights come from?" The correct answer to that question is they come from God. *All true rights come from God.*

There are three major considerations which go into this answer. First is the testimony of Scripture itself. The Bible attributes the existence of rights to God, and we will examine what the Bible teaches about rights in this chapter. The second consideration has to do with our definition of a right as being the just power to make a moral claim upon someone. Only the Christian worldview can truly account for the existence of a just power. Since the concept of justice requires a fixed, absolute moral standard, rights can only come from the Christian worldview. The Christian worldview can make sense of fixed, absolute moral standards and justify their existence.

---

31   For those interested in the historical development of rights theories within Christian theology, I recommend Gary Amos, *Defending the Declaration: How the Bible and Christianity Influenced the Writing of the Declaration of Independence,* (Brentwood, Tennessee: Wolgemuth and Hyatt, 1989), and Brian Tierney, *The Idea of Natural Rights: Studies on Natural Rights, Natural Law, and Church Law, 1150-1625,* (Grand Rapids, Michigan: William B. Eerdmans, 1997).

Secular systems such as legal positivism cannot account for the conditions necessary for genuine rights to exist. This inadequacy is the third consideration in our answer to the question, "Where do rights come from?" This will be explored in chapters five and eight.

A foundation for human rights is embedded in the first verse of the Bible: "In the beginning, God created the heavens and the earth" (Genesis 1:1). Anything which exists owes its existence to God. God is the owner of the universe because He created it:

> *In His hand are the depths of the earth; the heights of the mountains are His also. The sea is His, for He made it, and His hands formed the dry land. Oh come, let us worship and bow down; let us kneel before the LORD, our Maker! For He is our God, and we are the people of His pasture, and the sheep of His hand.*
>
> Psalm 95:4-7

God is an owner of property. It is His by right. No human law created or bestowed that right upon Him. The right to own property is a basic human right and the foundation of that right is God's ownership of the universe.

How do we get from God's right to own property to man having that right? Man has the right to own property because he is authorized to act in that capacity on behalf of the ultimate owner, God. In Genesis 1:26-28, God created man in His image. The image of God in man entails many things, including the ability and the authority to own property. The text says:

> Then God said, "Let us make man in our
> image, after our likeness. And let them have
> dominion over the fish of the sea and over the
> birds of the heavens and over the livestock
> and over all the earth and over every creeping
> thing that   creeps on the earth." So God
> created man in His own image, in the image
> of God He created him; male and female He
> created them. And God blessed them. And
> God said to them, "Be fruitful and multiply
> and fill the earth and subdue it and have
> dominion over the fish of the sea and over
> the birds of the heavens and over every living
> thing that moves on the earth."
>
> Genesis 1:26-28

Notice that man is commissioned by God to rule. This is what theologians refer to as the "dominion mandate." Man exercises dominion over creation on behalf of God, operating as a steward of what has been entrusted to him by the Creator. This is man's duty and it is his right.[32]

Property rights are clearly recognized in Scripture. Therefore, to steal another person's property is a sin (Exodus 20:15). Have you ever truly reflected on the concept of property? If I go to the store and purchase

---

32 Although many elements of the modern environmental movement are misguided and end up devaluing both God and man, the core impulse to act as stewards of the creation comes from having the image of God implanted in the human heart. After sin entered the picture in Genesis 3, man's stewardship of creation (and of rights) became problematic.

a pair of shoes, they come under my ownership. My neighbor is not entitled to them, and it is wrong for him to take them against my will. But why is it wrong? Does the concept of ownership comport with reality? If you are walking along a public beach and find a pretty shell which you pick up and take home with you, is it now *your* shell? Why is it yours and not mine? Or is it? In his *Second Essay Concerning Human Government*, John Locke (1632-1704) argued that the very concept of property depends upon God who created the world and then gave Adam and his descendants the mandate to take dominion over it (see Locke's *Second Essay*, Chapter V).

If a law were passed tomorrow which required you to turn over all your possessions to a central government and also decreed that private property was abolished, would you accept that law as being a just power? A mother has a favorite crayon drawing given to her by her five-year-old daughter. The picture must be turned over to the government, because by law the crayon and the paper belong to the government. Does that mother have a property right to the picture drawn for and given to her by her daughter? Does the daughter even have the right to give it to her mother (a transfer of ownership)? Can a universe without God provide any true foundation for abstract concepts such as rights, justice and property? No. But from its very first chapters, the Bible provides the foundation upon which we all depend, even those among us who will not admit it.

Because man is created in the image of God, to murder someone is a crime against God:

From his fellow man I will require a reckoning for the life of man. "Whoever sheds the blood of man, by man shall his blood be shed, for God made man in His own image."

Genesis 9:5B-6

Can we conclude that our duty to God not to murder a fellow human means that person has a right to life? Yes. His right to life is inherent on the basis of his bearing the image of God.[33] If man did not bear the image of God, he would not possess that right. The key to understanding this is the meaning of a right as being inherent. The concept of inherent rights makes no sense if man is the result of naturalistic evolution – an unplanned collection of molecules which form a biological thing. This happened by accident, and is the end result of billions of years of chance and random mutations lacking in intelligent design or transcendent purpose. So it makes no sense to talk about inherent rights in the context of a chance universe which entirely consists of matter in motion.

Several years ago, my children raised chickens. One night a fox (or two) managed to get into the coop and kill all but one chicken. My children were upset, but the fox was simply acting upon its instincts. We don't look at that incident in terms of whether or not the fox violated the rights of the chickens. To talk about a rights dispute between a chicken and a fox is nonsense, because

---

33 The term "inherent," as used here, means something that is essential or intrinsic to being human. It is a part of who we are. An inherent right is not something we bestow on people; it is something they are born with.

what happened was simply a function of nature. But if man owes his existence to the same accidental forces of naturalistic evolution as the fox and the chicken, then there is no reliable foundation for believing in human rights. However, it does make sense to talk about rights because the universe is not what the atheist says it is. God exists.[34]

God is a property owner and a rights-holder and He created man in His image so that man can fulfill the dominion mandate. This is foundational to rights, but the Bible has much more to say. The Old Testament is filled with commands to act justly and to treat others with justice (see Exodus 23:2, 6, 9; Leviticus 19:15; Deuteronomy 24:17; Jeremiah 21:12. These are but a small sampling of a much larger body). Isaiah 10:1-2 says:

> *Woe to those who decree iniquitous decrees,*
> *and the writers who keep writing oppression,*
> *to turn aside the needy from justice and to*
> *rob the poor of my people of their right, that*
> *widows may be their spoil, and that they*
> *may make the fatherless their prey!* [35]

The word "justice" is related to the concept of righteousness. When the Bible says that God is righteous, it means that God's very nature and character is righteous and that He is the standard of righteousness against which everything else is measured. Together, the justice

---

34   A case for the existence of God will be presented in Chapter 6: "Yes, God Exists."

35   Remember, we are reading an English translation of Hebrew Scripture. It is helpful to read a variety of translations, especially when dealing with concepts such as rights and justice.

and righteousness of God provide the only foundation for a genuine understanding of human rights. Justice is therefore a norm imposed by God and required of people in their relationships with each other. I believe that the justice God requires of one person implies the existence of a right on behalf of the person to whom that justice is due. It is not simply that we have God-given duties (we certainly have those), but that we also have God-given rights.

The concepts of justice and rights are both expressed by the Hebrew word "mishpat" in various contexts in the Old Testament. Mishpat is a very rich word and functions in a variety of ways, a full description of which goes beyond the scope of this book. But central to the idea of mishpat is the establishment and preservation of justice. In the Old Testament Jewish community, it was incumbent upon judges to see that mishpat was upheld in courts and in the rulings that were made in those courts.

Should we expect to find in the Old Testament modern Western terminology and concepts exactly as we know and use them? No. We are dealing with two very different cultures and languages separated from each other by thousands of years. However, based on what we read in Romans 2:14-15 (God has written His law on the human heart), we should expect to see similarities, and that is exactly what we find. In *An Introduction to Rights,* William Edmundson makes this observation:

> The presence or absence of a word or concise
> phrase or locution in another language, with
> which to translate a word we use, is hardly

conclusive as to the *availability* of an idea to speakers of another language. The Greeks had no word for *quarks*, but the idea of what a quark is could surely have been conveyed to them as a kind of constituent of certain subatomic particles – after all, we have borrowed the Greek terms *atomos, electron, proton* and so on in order to describe these very things. So, if the argument is that the concept of rights cannot be attributed to a linguistic culture lacking a precisely equivalent term, the argument is not a very good one.[36]

As noted, the concepts of justice and rights are both contained in the Hebrew mishpat in various contexts in the Old Testament. Human rights are a manifestation of the justice (mishpat) which is rooted in God's character. Because God is a rights-holder and because He created man in His own image, man has certain inherent properties that translate into duties (to act justly) and rights (to be treated justly). This proposition is not an alien concept that is illegitimately imposed upon the Old Testament.

For example, we see rights functioning in Jeremiah 32:6-7. At this time in Israel's (Judah) history, the Babylonians had conquered and controlled land owned by Jeremiah's family. God wanted the prophet Jeremiah to know that there was still a future for Israel, so God commanded Jeremiah to purchase the family land as a

36   William Edmundson, *An Introduction to Rights* (Cambridge: Cambridge University Press, 2004), pp. 5-6.

promise of future restoration:

> *Jeremiah said, "The Word of the LORD came*
> *to me: Behold, Hanamel the son of Shallum*
> *your uncle will come to you and say, 'Buy*
> *my field that is at Anathoth, for the right of*
> *redemption by purchase is yours.' "*

God commanded Jeremiah to follow the provisions of the law regarding land ownership within an extended family. To obey this was Jeremiah's duty, but he fulfilled that duty by exercising his God-given right (mishpat) of purchasing and owning the land. A similar concept is contained in the Hebrew word "din."[37]

The New Testament also provides a foundation for rights. We have already made reference to John 1:12 and its conferring of the right to be God's children upon those who acknowledge Jesus Christ as Lord and Savior. The Greek word used for right in John 1:12 is "exousia," which means authority or the right to control.[38] It is the word used in Romans 9:21, *"Has the potter no right...?"* God has the authority or the right (exousia) to control the clay.

The relationship of authority to rights in the New Testament is very significant. On what basis can one human being really have authority over another human being? Unless there is a higher authority (God) who

---

37 Din is connected with the concept of justice and rights being honored in the legal judgments of those appointed to serve as Israel's legal judges. It is the word used for rights in Proverbs 31:8-9.

38 Kenneth Wuest translated exousia in this verse as "legal right," based upon his study of first-century usage. Wuest said it meant that a person was given the legal right to do or be something. See Kenneth S. Wuest, *Wuest's Word Studies From the Greek New Testament*, Volume III, "Golden Nuggets," (Grand Rapids, Michigan: William B. Eerdmans Publishing Company, 1973), p. 94.

delegates His authority to others, there is no real basis for believing one human being or a group of human beings has authority over another person or persons. You might have power over me and might be able to force my compliance or punish me for being non-compliant to your wishes, but does that strike you as reflecting a genuine existence of authority? We think of genuine authority as having some sort of moral sanction, something that transcends the mere exercise of superior force.

Suppose I were to point a loaded gun at your head and demand that you give me your wallet. Do I have the authority to do that? No, not by any reasonable definition of the word authority. Do I have the power to take your wallet? I do, thanks to my possessing a loaded gun. It goes back to our definition of a right as "a just power to make a moral claim upon someone." It is not enough to have power; it must be a just power or there is nothing moral about the claim. Exercising power without genuine authority is not a right, it is tyranny. Any claim to authority a person might make that is not contingent on a higher authority (God alone is a sufficient higher authority) is not just and it is not a right. Having a majority (or a gun) on your side gives you might, but it does not make you right!

The truth of the matter is that without God all forms of human government are, at their core, exercises in tyranny. They may not seem tyrannical to those in power or to those who believe that the government is generally beneficial to their interests, but given the right circumstances, even those who have received some benefit will experience tyranny. Fortunately, God is involved in human affairs and there is a biblical foundation for human government. Romans 13:1-5 instructs the individual concerning his duty to government. Once again, we see the significance of exousia (authority). The first two verses say:

> Let every person be subject to the governing authorities. For there is no authority except from God, and those that exist have been instituted by God. Therefore whoever resists the authorities resists what God has appointed, and those who resist will incur judgment.[39]

The biblical worldview provides a foundation which simultaneously establishes the right of governments to rule and the rights of individuals.[40] In both cases, rights are ultimately contingent upon God.

So far, we have looked at biblical data in our search for a true foundation for rights. There is another branch of Christian theology called "natural theology," and this can also be useful in the quest for a transcendent foundation for rights. As a matter of fact, the majority of Christian writings on rights deal more with general revelation than

---

39   Although some translations refer to "power" as opposed to "authority," the English word authority comes closer to reflecting the meaning of exousia in this context.

40   In many ways, the Declaration of Independence was written as a theological argument to explain why the American Colonies were not rebelling against God when they stepped out from under the authority of King George III and Parliament. Whether or not the argument was biblically sound is debatable, but the Signers wanted to make clear that they did not intend to reject God's authority. Although Thomas Jefferson was the primary author of the Declaration of Independence, he had to produce a document that 55 other men would be willing to sign, and most of them were professing Christians.

with special revelation.[41] Related to natural theology, but not identical to it, are natural law and natural rights.

Let's start with natural law. Natural law is the theory or belief that some laws are basic to human nature and exist apart from any man-made law or positive law.[42] These laws have a moral quality to them and are considered to be part of the fabric of human nature and the universe. Because these laws exist independently of and prior to man-made positive law, they can be discovered. Unlike material things, natural law is not discovered through an instrument such as a microscope or telescope, but through the instrument of human reason. The ancient Greeks and Romans took natural law very seriously.[43]

Along with natural law, we encounter the concept of natural rights. Like natural law, natural rights reflect something about the very nature of man, something that stands apart from and above mere legal rights (rights

---

41 General revelation is the knowledge of God that has been universally available throughout human history. It comes through God's creation (Romans 1:18-20), the human moral conscience (Romans 2:14-15) and God's providence in history (Acts 14:15-17). Natural theology refers to the theological propositions arrived at through the use of human reason interacting with general revelation. God, in His common grace, has provided general revelation to all cultures throughout history, enabling people to be civil and to build civilizations. This is possible even when knowledge of the true God is limited, suppressed and distorted.

42 "Positive law" is the term given to laws which are made, enacted or "posited" by man. Positive law is not discovered or arrived at by human reason as though it existed outside of man. Positive laws are the laws made by man, and these laws are conditioned by history and are subject to change.

43 The Christian concept of natural law and natural rights recognizes that God created the universe and human nature with certain moral traits that can be discovered without the special revelation of Scripture. Nevertheless, it is still God who makes this knowledge possible. Within the history of philosophy there is a secular version of natural law and natural rights that does not depend on God, it simply accepts natural law and natural rights as being ingrained in the universe. This secular version was prominent during the period known as The Enlightenment (1600-1800), but it has been rejected by many contemporary secularists and replaced by legal positivism.

brought into existence by the writing of a positive law). Natural rights are protections possessed by the individual within an organized society. However, they are his by virtue of being human, not because society grants them.

The existence of natural law and natural rights explains how human beings have been able to form societies and civilizations for thousands of years. Whether or not the various civilizations recognized or understood this concept, natural law and natural rights are a reflection of the general revelation of God and His common grace.[44] As Paul wrote in Romans 2:14-15, people know by nature the things required by God's law. This is true even for those who do not have the written law of God (the Bible), because God has written His law upon their hearts. We have previously noted the words of C.S. Lewis:

> These, then, are the two points I wanted to make. First, that human beings all over the earth have this curious idea that they ought to behave in a certain way, and cannot really get rid of it. Secondly, that they do not in fact behave that way. They know the Law of Nature; they break it. These two facts are the foundation of all clear thinking about ourselves and the universe we live in.
>
> *Mere Christianity, p. 7*

We began this chapter by asking where in the

---

44 "Common grace" is a term which describes the kindness and mercy God has shown to the whole human race, despite its fallenness, ingratitude and rebellion. God causes the rain to water the crops of the ungodly (Matthew 5:45). God restrains sin in the human race enough so that we can have civilizations. Common grace is described in Acts 14:16-17.

Bible one can find this verse: "And God said, 'Let there be rights, and there were rights'" While a verse with that exact wording does not exist, the Bible does provide a foundation for rights and does answer the second of our original three questions: "Where do rights come from?" Rights come from God.

Chapter Five:

Wrong About Rights

Throughout this book, we are asking three basic questions and we are using the Christian worldview to answer them. The questions are:

1) What is a right?
2) Where do rights come from?
3) How do you know?

In the preceding chapter, we answered the second question: "Where do rights come from?" with: "Rights come from God." This answer makes perfect sense within the Christian worldview. Admittedly, my answer also presupposes the existence of God, something atheists and many legal positivists will contest. Consequently, at some level, this book must serve as an apologetic for the existence of God. That will be the focus of Chapter Six: "Yes, God Exists." In the present chapter we will consider how secular theories attempt to answer our three questions about rights, and we will see how those who embrace secular theories are wrong about rights.

When Charles Darwin published his *Origin of Species* in 1859, it rapidly accelerated a major intellectual revolution that was taking place in the Western world. It caused people to believe that the power of biological evolution and natural selection could account for life on purely naturalistic grounds. The need to rely on supernatural explanations (God) to deal with the previously indecipherable mystery of life and origins was no longer necessary. While some people might try to retain the supernatural by saying that Darwin was simply explaining how God operates in nature, the driving intellectual force behind the spread of Darwinism was naturalistic (non-supernatural) in emphasis. Naturalistic evolution became an umbrella under which other fields of academic research would begin to operate.

How are law and human rights to be understood now that they are both under the shadow of Darwin's umbrella? Like biological life itself, man's intellectual activities are the result of the same naturalistic processes that are at work in nature. Since man is the product of an unplanned process, the activities, behaviors and beliefs of man are also the result of the accidental forces of nature. This includes man's activities as a lawmaker and as a social being. It is the blind forces of naturalistic evolution that give man his nature. Man is not created in the image of God. There is no unchanging, universal "human nature," there is no natural law and there are no natural rights. There is no God to endow man with rights that are inherent to being human.

Think for a moment about bees and ants. Both have social structures that allow them to cooperate within their respective species. Their ability to cooperate enables them to survive, to reproduce and to perpetuate the hive or the colony. We do not think in terms of them as having rights. When a colony of ants overruns another colony and kills or enslaves the weaker colony, the dominant colony is simply functioning according to the way in which they have evolved. There is no moral factor or rights violation. To introduce morality or rights upon the behavior of ants is to impose an artificial concept upon them. The "laws of nature" that govern their behavior have no moral quality. The ants are simply acting according to the way in which the naturalistic process of evolution has created them. The same is true for bees. So why should we not view people the same way?

In the Christian worldview, law and rights are closely connected to morality and ethics. In the preceding chapter, we examined the biblical data and saw the direct link between God's righteousness and justice, and the corresponding duties and rights of men. Within the Christian or biblical worldview, rights and morality swim in the same pool. God is the ultimate reference point for our standards of morality, the justness of our laws and the exercise of our rights. These things are not ultimately the subjective inventions of man, a being that, according to Darwin, is constantly evolving and changing. Because of God, there is an objective (external to man and universal in scope) foundation for morality/ethics, law and human rights.

Every thinking person has ethical sensitivities and a belief that some things are right and other things are wrong. And we all have moral values. Because morality is such a central concern to humanity, any worldview which wants to be taken seriously must be able to supply a cogent account for it. In giving such an account, a worldview's theory of rights will inevitably be displayed as well.

A moral consensus exists that if a fifty-year-old man kidnaps his neighbor's four-year-old daughter, rapes and tortures her for his sadistic pleasure, and then murders her to avoid detection, he has committed a moral wrong. What he has done entails more than just breaking some written standard in a local community's criminal law. If he had attacked this child on an unpopulated island where no written law existed, a "law" would still have been violated.[45] Most importantly, the little girl deserved better treatment. There is something about her, something intrinsic to her personhood against which this man has committed a great injustice. Something more than a legal code has been violated; the little girl had a right which was transgressed by the man.

If there is no God, how would one begin to construct an argument for the moral values, laws and rights one wishes to accept? From an atheistic or secular viewpoint, the most promising basis upon which a secular ethical and legal system can be built is biological evolution. Using the template of natural selection, one can make the argument that there is something about the brain's capacity to think in ethical terms that enhances survivability. Therefore,

---

45 A universal moral law, God's law, exists and is just as obligatory on this isolated island as it is in any populated community that operates under written laws.

these particular genetic traits of the brain are passed down to succeeding generations and over millions of years, they increase in complexity. Ethics (and human rights which come from those ethics) are simply products of brain functions which have evolved over great spans of time.

One of the leading proponents of evolutionary ethics is Dr. Michael Ruse. Some readers might recognize his name because of his public and highly visible opposition to Intelligent Design's being taught in public school science classrooms.[46] But Dr. Ruse is also one of the world's most accomplished philosophers and he has been at the forefront of the school of thought which seeks to join biology and ethics. His position is summarized in his essay, *Evolutionary Ethics: A Defense.*[47]

Dr. Ruse contends that "humans are kinds of animals that benefit biologically from cooperation within their groups" (p. 96). That proposition does not seem to be controversial. Social cooperation can certainly enhance one's physical well-being. The problem is in what follows:

> To make us cooperate for our biological ends, evolution has filled us with thoughts about right and wrong, about the need to help our fellows, and so forth. We are obviously not totally selfless. Of course, our normal disposition is to look after ourselves; we have to do that if we are to reproduce. However, it is in our biological

---

46 Michael Ruse appeared in Ben Stein's 2008 documentary film, *Expelled: No Intelligence Allowed.*

47 Michael Ruse. *Evolutionary Ethics: A Defense in Biology, Ethics, and the Origin of Life,* edited by Holmes Ralsten III, (Boston: Jones and Bartlett Publishers, 1995).

interests to cooperate. Thus we have evolved innate mental dispositions (what the sociobiologists Charles Lumsden and Edward O. Wilson call "epigenetic rules") inclining us to cooperate in the name of this thing called morality (pp. 96-97).[48]

In Dr. Ruse's worldview, biological evolution is the foundation of all life and therefore, every function of the biological life forms known as human beings has some connection with the process of evolution. Since some of the functions or behaviors of humans are to form societies, make moral judgments, write laws and talk about rights, this must reflect something about how evolution has conditioned us to think. To Dr. Ruse and others in his camp, this account of the origin of morality seems reasonable. But Dr. Ruse recognizes that we normally think of ethics and morality as having two layers of concerns. First, there is the normative or substantive component. Ethics describe or prescribe what actions to take and what not to take. This layer could be called the "what" of ethics; it tells me what I should do.

The second layer has to do with our tendency to ask the "why" about ethics. What are the foundations or justifications for ethical descriptions? You have told me what I should do, but can you explain to me why one action is morally superior to another? And, remember, the way in which someone answers these questions will have direct bearing on the foundations for human rights. Dr.

48 Have you ever noticed how evolutionists routinely speak of evolution as though it were a conscious thing, filled with wisdom and the purpose to design life?

Ruse does not run away from the second-layer question of why. He observes:

> The evolutionist's case is that ethics is a collective illusion of the human race, fashioned and maintained by natural selection in order to promote individual reproduction ... what is really important to the evolutionist's case is the claim that ethics is illusory in as much as it persuades us that it has an objective reference. This is the crux of the biological position. (page 101)

Dr. Ruse has openly admitted that there is no objective basis or reference for evolutionary ethics. For Dr. Ruse, ethics are purely subjective manifestations of human feelings or sentiments which have been formed by the process of naturalistic evolution. This view has many disturbing implications for human rights. To his credit, Dr. Ruse directly faces the implications of his position. He goes on to say:

> There are good biological reasons why it is part of our nature to objectify morality. If we did not regard it as binding, we would ignore it. It is precisely because we think that morality is more than mere subjective desires that we are led to obey it. (page 102)

This type of thinking is very destructive of human rights, and it is in error.[49]   Dr. Ruse is saying that because there is no God who has created us, there are no objective grounds for morality. However, he acknowledges that deep down inside we have some kind of innate awareness that objective moral values exist. Dr. Ruse assures us that it is a good thing to believe in objective morality, because this belief influences our behavior, causing us to treat others in such a way that allows us to have social cooperation. Of course, we now realize that evolution has played a trick on our minds. There is no objective morality (and this directly implies that there are no objective human rights), but what a helpful illusion it is for us to believe that there is! After all, if the illusion were not so convincing, none of us would choose to obey the moral codes necessary for social cooperation and for respecting human rights.

If someone were to take Dr. Ruse's view of naturalistic evolution and subjective morality and apply it to law and human rights, what sort of legal system would result? There would be many options, because once we deny the existence of an objective standard that is universal and unchanging, anything goes. Hitler's Germany, Stalin's Soviet Union and Mao's China would all be equally valid. And should someone object to the mass extermination of millions of people, we would assure them that morality is really an illusion foisted on us by evolution. There is no objective standard of justice and righteousness by which those systems could be judged to be in error. Inherent

49 My reason for calling it error is that I believe simply disagreeing with something or not liking it does not count as a refutation. I think Dr. Ruse's position opens the door to terrible human rights abuses, but that does not mean he is wrong. His position needs to be refuted (see Chapter Six: "Yes, God Exists").

human rights? Just part of the illusion. Natural law and natural rights? There is no room for them in a universe which exists by accident and without design or ultimate purpose.

Harvard Law School Professor of Law Alan Dershowitz does his best to demonstrate how there can be a meaningful system of human rights in an atheistic universe. His book, *Rights From Wrongs: A Secular Theory of Rights,* deserves to be taken seriously because of his eminent stature in legal and academic circles. Dr. Dershowitz has the same basic view of man's origin and development as does Dr. Ruse. As a trained legal scholar, Dr. Dershowitz has attempted to develop a legal theory consistent with his beliefs. He has stated:

> We are creatures of accidental forces who have no pre-ordained destiny or purpose. We must make our own destiny and determine our own purposes. (page 31)

> And the implications of experience for "truth" are neither static nor self-evident. Experience, morality, legality, even truth are ever-changing, always-adapting, constantly interacting with nature and nurture. (pages 33-34)

> Likewise with the quest to satisfy the need for an external source of basic rights: The difference is that we will never find the latter, because it does not exist. Just as

human beings created an intervening God, organized religion, and the after life, so, too, have we created divine natural law, secular natural law, and other moral and legal fictions deemed essential to satisfy some of our most basic and enduring needs. (page 61)

We cannot endure without morality, law and rights, yet they do not exist unless we bring them into existence. (page 79)

Just like Dr. Ruse, Dr. Dershowitz believes that man exists by accident, the result of billions of years of unplanned, purposeless events occurring within a universe that is just as accidental, unplanned and purposeless. If that is the nature of man and of the universe, then to talk about rights as being anything other than figments of our imaginations makes no sense, and to talk about morality being anything other than the subjective preferences of people makes no sense, either. After all, people are prone to change their minds, their values and their beliefs as soon as the next wave of mutations affects the synaptic firings of their brain neurons and works its way into the genetic code. Because all these things are so (according to Dr. Dershowitz), it is we who bring morality, law and rights into existence. That does mean, of course, that we can also remove morality, law and rights from existence.

Having said all these things about morality, law and rights being man-made and fluid, Dr. Dershowitz will nevertheless insist that some things are truly and absolutely wrong and immoral. Dr. Dershowitz loudly protests that he is an atheist and that morality is a human invention, but he cannot avoid the law which, according to Romans 2:14-15, God has written on the human heart, including Dr. Dershowitz's heart. Do the following quotes from Dr. Dershowitz's same book strike you as the words of someone who believes we invent a morality which is constantly changing and relative to place and time?

God's law has been the source of justification for genocidal crusades, inquisitions, slavery, serfdom, monarchy, anti- Semitism, anti-Catholicism, bigotry against Muslims, genocide against Native Americans, homophobia, terrorism, and **many other wrongs.** (page 24)

It insults God to believe that it was He who mandated eternal inequality for women, execution for gays, slavery, animal sacrifice, and the scores of immoral laws of the Bible, the Koran, and other books purported to be speaking in God's name. Humans falsely speaking in God's name are to blame for **these immoralities** ... (page 26)

... the Holocaust, slavery, and the genocide against Native Americans were **unmitigated evils** by any meaningful definition of that term ... Human beings should do everything in their power to prevent recurrence of these and other wrongs, and the first step is to **recognize them as wrongs**. (pages 30-31);

(emphasis added in above statements)

Throughout his book, Dr. Dershowitz reminds us that he is a moral relativist, yet over and over again, he writes as though he believes in moral absolutes. He is a bundle of contradictions. He denies the existence of objective moral absolutes and objective human rights, yet he is convinced that his standards are applicable to others. He believes that others are guilty of creating moral fictions, but he is not. He is sure that he possesses moral standards that he can use to determine that others are guilty of "wrongs," "immoralities," and "unmitigated evils."

How do we account for these glaring inconsistencies? Dr. Ruse has already provided the explanation. Do you remember what Dr. Ruse said? Ethics is a collective illusion of the human race, fashioned by evolution, and is illusory because it persuades us that it has an objective reference. Evolution has tricked us into believing that morality is more than mere subjective desires. But this illusion is fortunate, for it enables Dr. Dershowitz to believe that all the things he thinks are wrong actually are "immoralities" and "unmitigated evils," not merely his subjective personal preferences.

Dr. Dershowitz says that there is no God and that "we are creatures of accidental forces who have no pre-ordained destiny or purpose." And he looks favorably upon the words of Stephen Jay Gould, who said: "There is nothing special about us. The world is not here for us. We are not the object of creation, but rather the product of random forces."

(*Rights From Wrongs*, page 79)

In Dr. Dershowitz's universe, man exists by accident, he has no purpose or destiny and rights and morality do not exist on their own; rather, we invent them. But let someone invent a different moral code than one that Dr. Dershowitz approves of, and he will use absolutes to denounce the alternative system. Let someone invent a right that Dr. Dershowitz dislikes (such as the right to conduct the Holocaust against European Jews), and he will argue that a person does not have the right to invent that particular right.[50]

Overlooking his unintentional misrepresentation of the Bible (the previously cited quote from page 26 of his book), let us grant Dr. Dershowitz his assumption of the solely human origins of the Bible. Why should the ancient Hebrews be condemned for inventing their own morality, especially if it helped them create a society that they preferred over other possible alternatives? Dr. Dershowitz claims that morality is a human invention, yet he insists that some things are truly and absolutely wrong, that some things are "unmitigated evils" that

---

50   I agree with Dr. Dershowitz that the Nazis did not have the right to exterminate the Jews, but I have a worldview which can justify denying that the Nazis were operating within their rights. In the biblical worldview, true rights are not human inventions; but Dr. Dershowitz's worldview has no objective standard by which he can, with consistency, denounce the Nazis for inventing rights with which he personally disagrees.

could never be justified (see Romans 2:14-15). He seems unwilling to admit that his own morality is a mere human invention. He displays all the symptoms of someone who deep down inside knows that God exists, yet suppresses that knowledge (the phenomenon described in Romans 1:18-21).

How then does Dr. Dershowitz construct a theory of rights? Throughout this book, I have made mention of the system known as legal positivism. Legal positivism is the theory that dominates the teaching of law in America today. It is a secular theory that denies any supernatural foundation to law or any existence of rights apart from what is created by human positive law. Dr. Dershowitz does not consider himself to be a legal positivist. His rejection of legal positivism includes this reasoning:

> Rights *do not come from the law alone*, because if they did, there would be no basis on which to judge a given legal system. Rights *come from human experience*, particularly experience with injustice.
>
> (page 8, emphasis his)

I agree with Dr. Dershowitz that rights cannot come from the law alone, because we need a basis for judging any given legal system. Without that basis, we would not be able to judge a legal system which grants men the legal right to rape women who wear blue jeans in public. But as we have seen, Dr. Dershowitz cannot himself escape the problem he has rightly diagnosed within legal positivism. Dr. Dershowitz wants to create rights that are responsive to injustice. He chose the title *Rights From Wrongs* for his book. He believes that as we identify wrongs and injustices such as slavery, genocide and religious oppression, rights ought to be created to prevent those wrongs. Unfortunately, Dr. Dershowitz has repeatedly told us that morality and rights do not exist unless we create them. He preaches moral relativism, but refuses to live with the results of relativistic thinking that some other people profess. He wants to have it both ways. He wants to be permitted to call certain things injustices, even if those who commit these acts do not agree with Dr. Dershowitz' claim that their actions are unjust.

Dr. Dershowitz condemns genocide yet he supports a woman's right to abortion. Since he denies that there is any objective standard for morality and rights that is universal, absolute and eternal (and certainly there is no Divine standard), how do we determine that genocide is wrong but abortion   is not, or how do we even determine that abortion is not a form of genocide (infanticide)? It all comes down to politics. He writes:

> In any event, the reality is that rights are legal constructs devised by the minds of human beings, based on human experience, and they must be consistently defended in the court of public opinion. (page 8)

I cannot help but wonder if Dr. Dershowitz would accept the verdict of public opinion if 99 percent of Americans decided that Harvard law professors should be placed in concentration camps. I know he would not accept that verdict, that it would represent one of the "wrongs" he opposes. Of course, Dr. Dershowitz reserves for himself (and for those who think like him) the right to tell others that they are doing wrong even if those others think they are doing right. He writes:

> Since I do not believe that rights exist outside of human experience – they are not God-given, natural, or eternal – I can do no more than advocate them. I have always believed that the best defense of rights is an active and persistent advocacy rather than a passive recourse to "higher authority". Every day poses new challenges to entrenched ideologies and new opportunities to advocate rights. (page 9)

By now it should be clear that Dr. Dershowitz is lobbying for his personal preferences and he wants those preferences to be given the status of rights. He believes that those people who share his preferences are being reasonable and those who do not share his particular preferences are being unreasonable. Also, I suppose this means that the only people who should be allowed to create and bring into existence their own rights and their own morality are those who embrace the same particular illusion that Dr. Dershowitz does (that's assuming that Dr. Ruse is correct when he tells us that morality is an illusion placed in our minds by naturalistic evolution).[51]

---

51   My criticism of Dr. Dershowitz's method does not mean that I reject all of his moral values. I have no doubt that many of his moral values are commendable. The problem is that since he is a relativist, he cannot help but be arbitrary.

Both Dr. Ruse and Dr. Dershowitz are trying to construct a view of morality that reflects a universe which exists by accident, without design, and without transcendent purpose. This universe is constantly evolving and changing, and this includes man and his values. Dr. Dershowitz has tried to account for rights in a universe that he and Dr. Ruse agree has no room for objective morality and no room for God. The result is that they have unwittingly left us with two options, anarchy or tyranny.[52] Fortunately, the universe is not what they say it is. God exists.

---

52 These men would deny that they advocate anarchy or tyranny. My claim is that their systems provide no antidote to those two extremes. If they oppose anarchy, they will prevent it by imposing controls and restrictions that they invent, and the anarchist will be forced to comply. If they oppose tyranny, they will have to argue that the tyrant has no right to rule. Why not? Why can't the tyrant invent his own morality and award himself the right to rule as he pleases? On what basis does anyone have the right to rule? This problem will be discussed in Chapter Eight: "Secular Dreams and Nightmares."

Chapter Six:

Yes, God Exists

Does God exist? The answer that someone gives in response to this question will go a long way in determining his or her view of rights. The three questions at the heart of this book (What is a right? Where do rights come from? How do you know?) are largely an extension of a more foundational question, "Does God exist?" The Christian view of rights presupposes the existence of God. This chapter will provide a justification for that belief.

America has two conflicting histories of rights. In its early days, America was characterized by the belief that rights come from God. The Declaration of Independence attributed the rights to life, liberty and the pursuit of happiness to the Creator. America's founders did not hesitate to credit God as being the source of rights.

And can the liberties of a nation be thought secure when we have removed their only firm basis, a conviction in the minds of the people that these liberties are the gift of God? That they are not to be violated but with his wrath? Indeed, I tremble for my country when I reflect that God is just: that his justice cannot sleep forever.

> Thomas Jefferson,
> *Notes on the State of Virginia*,
> Query 18 (1781)

The fact that Jefferson was not an evangelical Christian does not diminish the fact that he based the existence of rights upon God. Alexander Hamilton expressed it this way:

> The sacred rights of mankind are not to be rummaged for among old parchments, or musty records. They are written, as with a sun beam in the whole volume of human nature, *by the hand of divinity itself*; and can never be erased or obscured by mortal power.[53]

The view of rights espoused by Jefferson and Hamilton that rights are rooted in God was almost universally accepted by their fellow Americans.[54]

---

53 Stephen F. Knott, *Alexander Hamilton and the Persistence of Myth*, (Lawrence, Kansas: University Press of Kansas, 2002), p. 16.

54 No claim is being made here that America's founders were people of impeccable character and untainted genius. Like us, they were afflicted with all the follies of a sin nature: lust, greed, prejudice, faulty logic, hypocrisy, etc. Nevertheless, a thorough study of their personal correspondence, public proclamations, the written minutes from political assemblies, the frequency of biblical quotes in their writings and a study of the sermons that were being preached in countless churches reveals that the founders and their generation were passionate in their conviction that rights depend upon God.

Today, the story is quite different. We have already noted the sentiments of Dr. Dershowitz and the widespread influence of legal positivism. What Dr. Dershowitz and legal positivism have in common is a shared aversion to basing rights on God. The contrast between America's founders and these contemporary legal scholars is significant and cannot exist in harmony with each other. Each position on rights excludes the other. The situation is like an old-fashioned showdown in a 1940's Hollywood B Western movie. Two gunfighters square off and one says to the other, "This town isn't big enough for the both of us!" The seasoned movie-goer knows that it is only a matter of time before the bullets start flying.

Which side is right? Here is where the question of God's existence takes front and center. If God does not exist then human rights, whatever they might be, do not come from God. Dr. Dershowitz's method of constructing a system of rights can still be debated, but his negative claim (rights don't come from God) is obviously true. On the other hand, if God does exist, then His character and His will are the foundation of all genuine rights and Dr. Dershowitz is utterly wrong.

Consider again our original three questions. The first question was, "What is a right?" Our answer is that a right is the just power to make a moral claim upon someone. The second question was, "Where do rights come from?" We answer that by saying that rights come from God. The third question was, "How do you know?" In a sense, this third question, when addressed to the Christian worldview, is asking, "How do you know God exists? You Christians say that a right is the just power to make a moral claim upon someone and that fundamental rights come from God and are found in His Word, but how do you know God exists?"

As already noted, the purpose of this chapter is to provide a justification for belief in the existence of God.[55] May I now state the obvious? Countless books, many of them numbering hundreds of pages, have been written to prove the existence of God, and equally lengthy books have been written against Him. How can we hope to adequately address the most important question in the universe within a few short pages? I'll cheat a little and extend this discussion into the next chapter as well (Chapter Seven: "Two Friends Talking"), but a basic case will be made in this present chapter.[56] I also encourage you to examine Appendices A and B. There, you will find transcripts from formal debates I have had with atheists.

One of the most effective presentations I know of which argues for the existence of God was made by Dr. Greg Bahnsen during his debate with atheist spokesman Dr. Gordon Stein. The debate was held on the campus of the University of California – Irvine in 1985.[57] Dr.

55   Remember, I am not arguing for a generic or undefined god; I am referring to the Christian God revealed in the Bible, the God of Abraham, Isaac and Jacob. God has given us the Bible as a means of knowing Him, and this includes knowing Him as the author of our rights.

56   A fuller treatment can be found in the author's book, *Ask Them Why: How To Help Unbelievers Find The Truth,* (Schaumburg, Illinois: Regular Baptist Press, 2007).

57   Copies of this debate are available in audio and written form, and I strongly encourage the reader to read or listen to the debate. It should also be noted that within eleven years of their debate, both Dr. Bahnsen and Dr. Stein passed away at fairly young ages. Dr. Bahnsen died in 1995 at age 47, and Dr. Stein passed away in 1996 at the age of 55. There could be no more sobering reminder of the importance of these matters.

Stein was an experienced speaker and was clearly very confident, both in his abilities and in the case for atheism. But when the debate had ended, I think all but the most biased of listeners would have agreed that Dr. Bahnsen's presentation was far more compelling than Dr. Stein's. What the audience heard that night was the *Transcendental Argument For God's Existence* (commonly referred to as TAG).[58] Years later, TAG continues to be a powerful argument for the existence of God. I believe that the content of TAG makes a unique contribution to the question of human rights. Indeed, I believe that TAG justifies the existence of God-given human rights in a way that surpasses other Christian approaches, and, more importantly, in a way which discredits non-Christian arguments against God-given rights.[59]

Before summarizing TAG and explaining its connection to America's debate about rights, we must sound a cautionary note about proof versus persuasion. It is possible to provide an argument for a truth claim that meets every reasonable standard for being a proof. But a legitimate proof might still leave someone unpersuaded. If the issue at hand is controversial and if someone has a personal stake in the matter (the issue of God's existence

---

58   The best written explanation of TAG is Dr. Bahnsen's own book, *Always Ready: Directions for Defending the Faith,* (Texarkana, Arkansas; Covenant Media Foundation, 1996).

59   Other Christian apologists choose different ways of arguing for the existence of God and the truth of the Christian worldview.   Some stress historical evidences for the miraculous resurrection of Jesus Christ or the irreducible complexity of even the simplest form of life as pointing to Intelligent Design.   Still others focus on the wonders of the Bible such as fulfilled prophecy.   For an overview of different options available to apologists, I recommend Stephen B. Cowan and Stanley N. Gundry, editors, *Counterpoints: Five Views on Apologetics* (Grand Rapids, Michigan: Zondervan, 2000).

is controversial and the personal stakes are incalculably high), then someone might choose to remain unpersuaded by an argument that is rationally incontrovertible.

Think of a man (we'll call him Ernest) who deeply loves his wife. He respects her and believes her to be of impeccable character and integrity. Ernest has made many personal sacrifices to help his wife achieve her goals. He thinks he knows everything about her, including how she spends her time when they are not together. One day his friend comes to him with a heavy heart to reluctantly report that he has discovered Ernest's wife is involved in an adulterous affair. Furthermore, this friend was able to take a picture of Ernest's wife walking into a hotel arm-in-arm with her boyfriend, and two more of Ernest's friends are willing to testify that they have seen similar things on other occasions. Although this evidence might seem damaging, and although more evidence might surface in the future, Ernest is resolute in his belief in his wife's virtuous character. He has made up his mind. His friends are either mistaken or they are lying. One thing is clear to him: It is time to find a new set of friends.

We saw this phenomenon described in Chapter Three, "The Stakes Are High." In his letter to the Romans, Paul explained that the truth of God's existence is already known by all people.[60] Nevertheless, people will try very hard to suppress what they know about God as a means of holding onto their autonomy and coping with their God-given moral conscience (Romans 1:18-21; Romans 2:14-15). An argument that leaves people unpersuaded

---

60 Paul was making a general statement about humanity. Obviously, he was not talking about an infant or a severely mentally challenged adult.

is not necessarily a flawed argument. Indeed, it may be a flawless argument that, all things being equal, proves the truth of a proposition. But when it comes to the human heart and its response to a holy and righteous God, all things are not equal (see John 6:44; Acts 4:13-22).

Having distinguished between proof and persuasion, let us now consider TAG. The core argument is this:

> The proof for the existence of God is that unless you presuppose His existence, you cannot prove anything at all.

At first glance, that argument can seem a bit strange. What does it mean to say that without God you cannot prove anything? After all, there are multitudes of atheists and they prove things all the time. Not only do they not presuppose the existence of God, they also openly deny His existence.

The key to understanding TAG is to understand the nature of presuppositions. Although all have presuppositions and make use of them on a daily basis, most people are not fully aware of what presuppositions are and how they operate. Actually, they are like breathing. We all breathe, but we rarely stop to think about it (unless struggling with a respiratory illness), and most of us have only a minimal understanding of the mechanics of breathing. Presuppositions are foundational beliefs upon which we build our knowledge of the world around us and interpret out experiences. It is helpful to think of these two components; "pre" and "suppose." To "suppose" something is to think or to know it. Pre means before. To presuppose, or to have a presupposition, is to think or know one thing before you think or know something else. John Frame defines it as follows: "A presupposition is a belief that takes precedence over another and therefore serves as a criterion for another. An ultimate presupposition is a belief over which no other takes precedence."[61]

Remember Ernest? He has a core belief in the moral integrity of his wife. This belief takes precedence over the testimony of his friends. Even when they produce physical evidence such as a picture of Ernest's wife walking into a hotel with another man, Ernest is not persuaded. Because he has presupposed the virtue of his wife, Ernest will look at that picture and conclude that his friends have altered it. Ernest's trust in his wife is not a fringe belief about a trivial matter. His friends are not trying to convince him that paintball deserves to be made an Olympic sport. Those kinds of beliefs can be modified or set aside without fundamentally affecting one's life, and so they don't dominate the way we see every thing else. Ernest's confidence in his wife is a core belief, and this core belief or presupposition controls his interpretation of the testimony and evidence presented by his friends.

A great example of the way in which presuppositions control our beliefs about God can be seen in comments made by atheist scholar Kai Neilsen during a debate with Christian apologist J.P. Moreland at the University of Mississippi. Regarding claims about the physical resurrection of Jesus, Dr. Neilsen said:

61   John Frame, The Doctrine of the Knowledge of God, (Phillipsburg, New Jersey: Presbyterian and Reformed Publishing, 1987), p. 45,

"Jesus, let us suppose – I don't know much about such things and to be perfectly frank, I'm not terribly interested in them, but let us just suppose it were the case that Jesus raised from the dead. Suppose you collected the bones, and they together in some way reconstituted the living Jesus. Suppose something like that really happened. Suppose there were good historical evidence for it. I have no idea if there is or isn't; I suspect for anything like that, there isn't very good evidence, but let us assume there is. This wouldn't show there was an infinite intelligible being. It wouldn't give you any way of being able to detect if there is a God. It would be just that a very strange happening happened, namely, that somebody who died – or certainly appeared to have died – came together again as a living human being."[62]

Dr. Neilsen's core presupposition is that the universe is naturalistic. There is no God and miracles cannot happen. We see John Frame's definition of a presupposition being illustrated by Neilsen. His presuppositional commitment to naturalism takes such precedence that even a physical resurrection from the dead, although it would be considered strange, would in no way indicate the existence of God. Neilsen would

62   J.P. Moreland and Kai Neilsen, *Does God Exist?* (Nashville: Thomas Nelson Publishers, 1990), p. 64

insist that there must be a naturalistic explanation, as yet undiscovered. I am not faulting Nielson for having presuppositions. We all have them, and knowledge would be impossible without them.

Another striking example of how presuppositions work can be seen in the *Humanist Manifesto II.*[63] In its assessment of religion, the *Manifesto* says:

> As nontheists, we begin with humans not God, nature not deity. Nature may indeed be broader and deeper than we now know, any new discoveries, however, will but enlarge our knowledge of the natural.

This is an atheistic presupposition at work. It insists that any future discovery, no matter what it is, will only add to our knowledge of the natural. The possibility of the supernatural is excluded in advance.

If presuppositions are so foundational that they take precedence over all other beliefs, how could they ever be shown to be false? It is true that we cannot test them directly, but we can approach them indirectly, or transcendentally.[64] This was the basis of Dr. Bahnsen's debate with Dr. Stein.

To explain TAG, Dr. Bahnsen would ask, "What

---

63   Paul Kurtz and Edwin H. Wilson, *Humanist Manifesto II,* (American Humanist Association, 1973).

64   I realize that the term "transcendentally" is a mouthful. Why not just call this argument PAG, "The Presuppositional Argument for God"? That would be fine with me, but there is a good reason for calling it TAG. The term "transcendental," as it is used in this context, refers to an analysis which asks what the preconditions are for the intelligibility (making sense) of human experience. People trust reason and sense experience (sight, sound, smell, taste, touch) to discover truth and attain knowledge. Transcendental analysis asks what must be presupposed, or what must already be true, in order for reason and sense experience to be accepted as reliable sources of knowledge.

are the necessary preconditions if there is to be any intelligibility for the laws of logic, the laws of science, and morality?" In other words, what does the universe have to be like in order for us to expect that there would even be laws of thought (logic), laws of science (which depend on induction and uniformity of nature), and moral absolutes? We all use those things everyday, and our use of them seems so natural that we rarely, if ever, stop to consider how we would justify using them. In order for us to justify making use of logic, science and morality, reality has to be something more than what the atheistic materialist says it is (matter in motion). A universe which is purely material in nature, existing naturally without design or purpose, could never provide the conditions we depend upon to use logic, science and morality.

In *Always Ready: Directions for Defending the Faith*, Dr. Bahnsen said it this way:

> Differing worldviews can be compared to each other in terms of the important philosophical question about the "preconditions of intelligibility" for such important assumptions as the universality of logical laws, the uniformity of nature, and the reality of moral absolutes. We can examine a worldview and ask whether its portrayal of nature, man, knowledge, etc., provide an outlook in terms of which logic, science and ethics can make sense. It does not comport with the practices of natural science to believe that all events

are random and unpredictable, for instance. It does not comport with the demand for honesty in scientific research, if no moral principle expresses anything but a personal preference or feeling. Moreover, if there are internal contradictions in a person's worldview, it does not provide the preconditions for making sense out of man's experience. For instance, if one's political dogmas respect the dignity of men to make their choices, while one's psychological theories reject the free will of men, then there is an internal defect in that person's worldview. [65]

"But wait just a minute," the atheist will protest. "Atheists are responsible for many scientific advances. We are certainly logical, and many atheists lead moral lives which surpass those of many professing Christians." TAG does not deny that atheists do those things. Quite the contrary: TAG asserts that atheists who use logic, science and morality are actually making the case for Christian Theism. In other words, by their actions, atheists are demonstrating that they do not live in an atheist universe, for such a universe (strictly material and existing without design) cannot justify the preconditions, or presuppositions, which are necessary if logic, science and morality are to be possible. Only a universe which has been created by God can provide the ground for the

65   Bahnsen, *Always Ready*, page 121.

things the atheist (and everyone else) does.

The God of Christian Theism is a thinking God (Romans 11:33-34), and the universe God created manifests the laws of logic, for these laws reflect how God thinks. God governs and sustains the universe He created (Colossians 1:16-17), therefore we can expect there to be consistency in the physical processes of the universe.[66] This provides the conditions necessary to think inductively and make use of empirical data, which in turn makes science possible. God is holy and unchanging in His moral character, thereby making possible the existence of moral absolutes. God has created mankind (male and female) to bear His image, thereby making possible the existence of human rights.

TAG asserts that it is impossible to prove anything at all unless you have already presupposed the existence of the God whose nature provides the basic tools necessary for doing logic, science and morality, and for constructing proofs.[67] Every system of thought begins somewhere with a foundational presupposition(s) by which other things are proven. But according to TAG, unless God Himself is that most basic or primary presupposition, any system of thought or any theory of knowledge will be internally inconsistent and lead to incoherence. When an atheist (or anyone who worships a god other than the God of Christian Theism) makes use of logic, science or morality he is using "borrowed capital." This means that the unbeliever is

---

66   Obviously, there are many processes we do not yet understand, and this can cause them to appear to us to be random and chaotic. However, it is with good reason that when we fill an ice cube tray with water and then put that tray in our freezer, we expect to end up with ice cubes.

67   The skeptic does not outwardly acknowledge God, but whenever he seeks to prove something, he is acting as though he lives in an orderly universe designed by God.

depending upon the Christian worldview even as he seeks to deny the truth thereof. This was masterfully portrayed by Dr. Bahnsen in his debate with Dr. Stein.

TAG reminds us that according to what we have already noted in Romans 1:18-19, people know that God exists and that He is eternal in nature and power. They give evidence of possessing this knowledge when they make use of logic, science, morality and universal human rights, all of which presuppose God. But they also give evidence to the phenomena of suppressing the truth of God as described in Romans 1:18-21. They do this when they outwardly deny the existence of God yet continue to borrow capital only He can supply.

As far as the charge that presupposing the existence of God is a blind leap of faith, or that it is unwarranted to presuppose something which first has to be proven, consider this: If I were to ask you to prove that logic exists, how would you do it? The moment you start to answer, you will be using logic (unless you speak in pure gibberish, "Blah blah blah blah blah."). I would interrupt your answer by saying, "Stop! You can't use logic in your answer until you first prove it exists. Prove it first, and then you will be warranted in using it." Are you starting to see why some things have to be presupposed before they can be proved? Perhaps you could stump me by saying, "I won't try to prove to you that logic exists because I don't believe in logic. I think logic is a myth." But once again, you would be employing logic even as you are professing not to believe in it! You would have to use logic to formulate your belief that logic doesn't exist.

The phenomenon of people borrowing capital from the Christian worldview is all around us and is easy to recognize, once you know what to look for. I remember the first time I watched the final Star Wars movie, *The Revenge of the Sith*. This was the episode that explained how Anakin Skywalker was seduced by the dark side of the Force and became Darth Vader. Near the end of the movie, Anakin's former master, Obi-Wan Kenobi, confronted him as they prepared to fight to the death. In rebuking Anakin, Obi-Wan said, "Only a Sith deals in absolutes." I was immediately struck by the inconsistency of Obi-Wan's criticism, for he made an absolute statement ("Only a Sith") in condemning Anakin's use of absolutes.

As Obi-Wan and Anakin fought their epic battle, they continued to argue. Finally, Obi-Wan said, "Anakin, Chancellor Palpatine is evil.". And that is the crux of the problem. The enlightened Obi-Wan had earlier insisted that only the Sith speak in absolutes, yet in order to condemn the evil Sith Lord, Darth Sidious (Emperor Palpatine), Obi-Wan had to use moral absolutes. He was borrowing capital from someone else's worldview. His own worldview could not account for the moral absolutes he was using to condemn Palpatine, yet he was convinced that his judgment was absolutely true.

The following chapter will provide a practical illustration of what TAG is and how people who are not professional philosophers, lawyers or theologians can use it in discussions about rights. Appendices A and B also illustrate how TAG can be used to explain the need for presupposing the existence of God. But presuppositions can be tested in secondary ways, as well (not just transcendentally). I believe that there are very impressive historical evidences for the bodily resurrection of Jesus Christ and for the divine inspiration of the Bible as evidenced by its fulfilled prophecies.[68] If the most basic presupposition of Christianity (God exists) is true, we would expect to find evidences of that presupposition which could be investigated empirically and historically. The Christian presupposition is not just a random choice or a blind leap of faith which could have just as easily been something totally different. No, we make God our starting point, because without Him you could not prove anything at all.

---

68 The apologetic method known as "evidentialism" emphasizes data from history, archaeology and science. While evidentialism can be a very fruitful line of inquiry, it is a different type of apologetic than TAG.

Chapter Seven:

Two Friends Talking

In order to help us understand the argument for God's existence that was offered in the preceding chapter, let's listen in on a conversation that covers that very ground. The Christian in this dialog is Drew, and he is 35 years old. He has been a Christian for ten years. Drew went to college to study business and received a degree in marketing. He has no academic training in philosophy, law or theology, but he is active in his church and attends weekly Bible studies. He also maintains a personal reading program. As you observe Drew in this conversation, it will be obvious that he has thought about these matters and that his church has done a good job discipling and equipping him with the Christian worldview.

If you are a Christian and have had minimal exposure to apologetics, Drew's conversation might seem out of reach and beyond what you think you can attain. I believe our churches are filled with people who could be like

Drew, but most churches offer very little or no training in basic apologetics. Furthermore, many Christian apologists completely ignore the need to produce quality, student-friendly curriculum that can be effectively taught in the local church. If such material were made available and pastors made use of it, then every church could have men and women like Drew. Not every Christian will be able to attain Drew's level of competence, but every Christian is commanded by Scripture to learn something about answering questions and sharing their testimony with non-Christians.

> ...but in your hearts, honor Christ the Lord as holy, always being prepared to make a defense to anyone who asks you for a reason for the hope that is in you; yet do it with gentleness and respect.
>
> (I Peter 3:15)

The non-Christian in this dialog is Neil, who is also thirty-five years old. Neil is a professing atheist who does not think that belief in God is reasonable. He is thoughtful and is willing to interact with his friend, Drew. Neil has no desire to play the role of "village atheist." In other words, Neil is not the sort who intentionally mocks Christianity while relying on simplistic or sarcastic arguments. During his childhood, Neil was not opposed to belief in God, it was simply something he seldom thought about. But as he went through high school and then on to college, Neil became sensitive to the suffering that exists in this world and the reasonable-sounding arguments he heard against God's existence. By the time he graduated from college with a degree in mathematics, Neil was convinced that God does not exist. In this dialog, Drew will be making use of the Transcendental Argument for God (TAG) described in the previous chapter. Drew will ask Neil to think about the role of presuppositions and what kind of universe we would need to live in if we are to take things like logic, morality and human rights seriously. After the conversation, a summary will be provided to further explain Drew's argument. Consider this conversation to be a prequel to a conversation they will have later about human rights and the gospel (Chapter Twelve: "Two Friends Talk Some More").

Neil: So let me get this straight. You're saying that belief in God is your starting point? That's about one step removed from fanaticism and the reason why Christianity can't be taken seriously by anyone who cares about facts and being rational. All you have done is to take a blind leap of faith.

Drew: Everybody has faith commitments at some level, Neil, including you. I am committed to God so that I can avoid blind leaps of faith. I don't use reason to get to God; I start with God and then reason my way out from there.

Neil: I suppose that makes you feel secure. After all, now you don't have to worry about all those annoying little facts that disprove the Bible. You can just pretend they don't exist. You've set this up so that it is impossible for anyone to reason with you. I mean, in a nutshell, here is your grand argument: "God said it, I believe it, and that settles it." Drew, your argument fits on a bumper sticker, and that's about all it is good for.

Drew: Neil, you just said that it is impossible for anyone to reason with me. The truth of the matter is this: If God didn't exist, it would be impossible for anyone to reason at all.

Neil: That doesn't make any sense. You don't need God to be able to reason. I don't believe God exists, yet I'm very committed to the use of reason. You can't prove God exists and, even if you could make a decent argument for God, you would still have no way of knowing that the Bible is his word. You're just making sweeping assumptions and you're arguing in a circle.

Drew: A kind of circle, yes. No one can completely avoid circles, Neil, including you, for that is the nature of how presuppositions influence our thinking. But circles, or presuppositions, can be tested and critiqued. Will you let me explain what I mean by this?

Neil: All right, go ahead. Give it your best shot.

Drew: Thanks. Now, the first thing I'm going to do is to ask you to assume, for the time being, that God exists ...

Neil: Stop! Drew, don't you get it? You first have to prove God exists and quit just assuming it.

And definitely don't ask me to assume it.

Drew: Neil, I need you to be willing to hear me out on this or we'll never get anywhere. How about this: Let's assume God does not exist and then consider the implications of a universe without God.

Neil: Run that by me again.

Drew: Instead of assuming or presupposing God, let's assume atheism. Now, there is no God so there is nothing supernatural. The natural universe is all that exists. There is matter and there is energy, or motion, but there is no one who has created, designed or guided the universe. It just is what it is – matter in motion. Now, assuming that is true, how do we get from that type of universe to what we actually experience in daily life? Each of us lives as though the universe is something far more than matter in motion.

Neil: What do you mean?

Drew: We live as though logic exists. How do we account for laws of thought in a purely material universe? How can logic come from non-logic? Then we will have to account for morality coming from non-morality, unless of course there is no morality. In an atheist universe we have life coming from non-life, reason coming from non-reason, rights coming from non-rights and order coming from randomness. If we really believe in the existence of purpose, logic, moral absolutes, love, beauty, justice and rights, how are these things possible in a universe which exists by accident and is ultimately just matter in motion? If these things are anything more than "make believe," what would the universe have to be like to account for them? These things are a vital part of human experience and you take them very seriously in your own life. You live as though logic, purpose, morality, love, beauty, justice and freedom truly exist and make a difference in your life.

Neil: I admit those things are big challenges for atheism, but they are equally big challenges for any worldview. My problem with what you're saying is that you are giving yourself a pass on the same challenge. You have not proven anything about God, you are simply assuming it.

Drew: In a sense, I'm assuming God exists, but that's okay, because you're assuming the exact same thing. You live as though you know God exists.

Neil: What's that supposed to mean? I resent your telling me what I believe, especially since you are implying that I am lying about not believing in God. Why don't you stick with your own beliefs and try to justify them, if you can!

Drew: Neil, I know you're struggling with my approach, but I think if you let me continue it will make sense.

Neil: Okay, try again.

Drew: Just like we assumed atheism and a purely

naturalistic universe and then compared it to real human experience, let's now assume Christianity and see how it fits with the existence of logic, moral values, purpose, love, beauty, justice, freedom and a whole host of similar things that impact our lives. According to the Christian worldview as explained in the Bible, God is the creator and sustainer of the universe. By His power the orderliness of the universe and its physical laws are maintained, and that's what makes science possible. God is a moral being with emotions, will and purpose, and He created us in His image with similar characteristics so that we might know Him and have a relationship with Him. God is the source and standard for things like justice, duty, beauty, love and human rights, and God created us with the capacity to experience those things. By the way Neil, may I ask you a question before I continue?

Neil: Sure.

Drew: What is the atomic weight of beauty?

Neil: Is that some kind of stupid trick question?

Drew: Well sort of, but I don't really think it's stupid. I could have asked what justice smells like or what the hardness of liberty is on the Mohs scale, or what color logic is. I know this sounds strange, because I am asking for the physical traits of non-physical things. We don't think of something like logic in terms of the five senses of sight, smell, hearing, taste and touch. But that's not a problem for the Christian worldview. We can account for all sorts of non-material or non-physical things that have genuine existence and they make sense in the Christian worldview.

Neil: Gotcha, Drew! You just shot yourself in the foot. All of those concepts or abstractions you just referred to correspond to brain activity. When you experience the sensation of beauty, we can detect a corresponding activity within your brain. There's no need to make some bogus appeal to a non-existent God. Human behavior is a matter of a biological organism interacting in a social and cultural context.[69]

Drew: If I raped your wife, murdered your children and burned down your house, would I be guilty of having done something morally wrong?[70]

Neil: Of course, that would be wrong.

Drew: If I had been connected to a device which measures brain activity during the time I was raping your wife and murdering your children, I have no doubt that something measurable would have been detected in my brain. End of story. The whole scenario would simply be external actions that resulted from or corresponded to activities in my brain. How

69   This sentence comes from *Humanist Manifesto II* (see Chapter Eight: Secular Dreams and Nightmares).

70   Neil knows Drew well enough to know that Drew would never make light of the serious and grievous nature of rape and murder. That something so serious would be used as an illustration is appropriate in this case, because no discussion could entail more important matters than the question of God's existence.

can an electro-chemical reaction in my brain be wrong or immoral? It's simply a matter of physics and chemistry. You might not personally like what I did to your family, but so what? In an atheist universe, morality doesn't really exist as an external standard that we are obligated to honor. My moral impulses are just a particular arrangement of molecules in my brain experiencing various electro-chemical reactions. The same is true of your moral impulses. When a scientist watches a chemical reaction take place in a test tube, he doesn't describe what he sees as being either moral or immoral. It's just chemistry and physics acting in accordance with the physical laws that operate in the universe. Why should a physical process in my brain that causes me to rape be viewed any differently than what happens in a test tube?

Neil: Come on, Drew, there's a huge difference and you know it.

Drew: Yes, Neil, you're right. There *is* a huge difference and we both know it, and that's because the universe is not what the atheist says it is. What we experience in this universe cannot be completely reduced to matter in motion. Of course the universe is material, God created it that way, but it includes far more than just the material. Of course the brain is a physical organ by which we think and engage the universe God created, but the human

	mind cannot be completely reduced to electro-chemical processes in the brain. If you deny this, then you have no genuine moral complaint when your wife is raped. But, Neil, you would have a genuine moral complaint because this is not an atheist universe.[71]
Neil:	You raised some interesting points, but at the end of the day none of what you said matters. You are guilty of embracing the biggest contradiction imaginable, a contradiction so serious that it sounds the death knell for Christianity. Furthermore, you walked right into it. I've been patiently listening to you, even though I knew the whole time that Christianity can't possibly be true and your own method of arguing makes the case for me.
Drew:	You have listened patiently and I appreciate it. I want to be just as patient and listen to you, Neil. I definitely don't want to embrace a contradiction, because in the Christian worldview contradiction is the hallmark of error. Would you be so kind as to show me my error?
Neil:	Well, to be honest with you, it is so obvious I'm surprised you don't already know it; but let me point it out to you. In your argument you asked me to assume that God exists and then to see how that fits with human experience. I know

71 Neil knows Drew well enough to recognize that Drew is not suggesting that atheists find rape and murder any less reprehensible than Christians do. Many atheists are very conscientious about how they treat the people around them.

	you believe that God is a loving God, correct?
Drew:	Absolutely.
Neil:	And God is all-powerful and all-knowing?
Drew:	Yes.
Neil:	Then how is this consistent with all the evil and

Neil: Then how is this consistent with all the evil and suffering we see? Why don't you come with me to visit the cancer wing at Children's Hospital? And when we get there, you can look at those parents and tell them about your loving God who is all-powerful and all-knowing. It doesn't add up. You used the illustration of rape to make a point. Well guess what? Rapes happen and God does nothing to stop them. If you had the knowledge that a rape was about to happen and you had the power to stop it and yet you did not intervene, no one in their right mind would ever have reason to think you were a loving person. Cruel, yes; loving, no. I know you, Drew, and I know you would risk your own life to stop that rape, yet you believe in and worship a God that would just let it happen, even knowing the needless hurt and trauma it would cause. You asked me to assume or presuppose that God exists and then see how that comports with or makes sense of what we experience in the universe. Well, I just showed you where that leads. Fortunately, there is no God, but if he did exist we could only conclude that he is cruel, unloving and uncaring. We are right back where we started; your belief in a loving God is a blind leap of faith and requires you to turn a blind eye to a huge contradiction.

Drew: You see, Neil, you do believe God exists! You do believe the universe is something far different than merely matter in motion.

Neil: Don't start with that garbage again.

Drew: Neil, we are still comparing universes. You say you believe in a universe without God and I believe that the universe was created by God. You just presented what philosophers, skeptics and theologians call "the problem of evil."[72] Fine, let's look at it. I hope to show you that by your very complaint against God, you demonstrate that deep inside your heart or mind you know that He exists. You know Him, but you are suppressing that knowledge. It shows up in a multitude of ways, however, no matter how hard you try to suppress it. This is especially evident in what you just said. Can I have just a couple of minutes to respond?

Neil: Yeah, but only if I can answer you back.

Drew: Fair enough. Do you remember Carl Sagan's famous book *Cosmos*?

Neil: A little; it came out a long time ago. I know someone made a television show out of it.

Drew: You're right, it was PBS. Anyhow, Sagan was a prominent astronomer and atheist and his book was quite a sensation. The very first chapter of his book had these words: "The cosmos is all that

72 See Chapter Ten: "Has God Violated Human Rights?"

is, or ever was, or ever will be."[73] Now, if that is true, why are you bothered by evil and on what basis can you even believe evil exists? Can you take me to a laboratory and show me evil under a microscope? Can you weigh it on a scale? Of course not, because the cosmos is all that is, or ever was, or ever will be. The Christian worldview can account for the existence of evil. You might not like the answer, but it does make sense within the Christian worldview. And Neil, I know something about you. When you talk about children with cancer or victims of rape, you are not just using a debate tactic. You are personally bothered by those things. They alert you to the fact that there is something wrong in this universe. Your complaint about evil was not just a tool to critique my presupposition that God exists; you were expressing your value system. You care deeply about the things you were complaining about, but if the universe is reducible to matter in motion and if the cosmos is all that is, or ever was, or ever will be, then cancer, rape and human life itself have no real significance except in your own mind. And your mind, your thoughts, your values and beliefs are nothing more than electro-chemical reactions in your brain operating according to the laws of physics. If you want to take the problem of evil seriously, you are going to have

73 Carl Sagan, *Cosmos* (New York: Random House, 1980) p. 1

	to borrow capital from my worldview, because in an atheist universe, not only does evil not matter, it doesn't even exist.
Neil:	You are the one who is running away from the issue, because you can't reconcile belief in an all-knowing, all-powerful, loving God with the cancer wing at Children's Hospital. Hey, I'll be the first to admit that I haven't figured out the universe yet; I'll plead ignorance. But you have embraced a massive contraction and you can't escape it.
Drew:	Once again, you're borrowing from my worldview in order to be able to reason or think about these things. This is further evidence that you know God, but you are suppressing the truth of His existence.
Neil:	How so?
Drew:	You accuse me of a contradiction. But what does the concept of "contradiction" require? A contradiction is a violation of a law of thought or a rule of logic. Do these rules or laws of thought actually exist?
Neil:	Of course, they do; we use them all the time.
Drew:	Are they material? I would like to look at one and hold it in my hand. Do you have one I can smell or taste?
Neil:	Here we go again. No, Drew, the laws of thought are not physical things; they are concepts we use, and we think of them in our brains.
Drew:	Then how can they be universal and objective?

Here's what I mean by that. By calling the laws of logic universal, we mean that they apply everywhere, to everybody, at all times. By calling them objective, we mean that they exist apart from any particular person. They're not individual preferences. In other words, they are not subjective, they are objective. We don't each make up our own laws of logic according to the particular processes in our brain. The laws transcend the individual and apply to everyone.

Neil: And your point is?

Drew: You have used the problem of evil to accuse me of embracing a contradiction. Now, I don't think the problem of evil presents Christianity with a genuine contradiction, but I'll temporarily assume that it does. What's to stop me from choosing a different set of logical laws than the ones you use? It would be like taking a math test and saying that two plus two equals seventeen. When my teacher marks my answer as incorrect, I'll simply say that according to my personal rules of math, two plus two does equal seventeen. You're free to adopt a set of rules that says two plus two equals four, but why can't I adopt a different set? Why can't I say that the rules of math are local and subjective, rather than universal and objective?

Neil: Because your math wouldn't work in the real world. You couldn't build a house or engineer an airplane or balance your checkbook using your own rules of math. You don't need to believe in God to figure out that two plus two equals four. It's just the way the universe works.

Drew: And logic works the same way?

Neil: If not identically, then at least similarly.

Drew: Then how can you account for universal, objective and non-material laws of thought in a universe that is merely matter in motion? Neil, you keep borrowing capital from my worldview. The Christian worldview can account for universal, objective and non-material laws, whether we are talking about laws of math, laws of science, laws of logic or laws of morality. That's why I can't invent my own laws of morality and use them to justify raping your wife and murdering your children. Obviously, I could make the claim that I can invent my own morality and say that morality is relative to the individual and is subjective, but you know in your heart that I would be wrong. There is a moral law God has written on both our hearts and it applies to everyone.

Neil: You're still ducking the problem of evil and the ignorance of believing in a loving God who permits childhood cancer.

Drew: Actually, Neil, I'm trying to show you where we agree. I do agree that if you could demonstrate a genuine contradiction, and not just an apparent contradiction, between the existence of evil and the existence of the Christian God, then I would have a huge problem on my hands. I am more than willing to explore that with you. But I'm trying to get you to recognize that you are using presuppositions that make no sense in an atheist universe. The very tools you are using, such as the laws of thought and the laws of morality, require that you presuppose a universe designed and created by God. You deny that He exists, but you depend on universals, absolutes and non-physical laws. Contradictions can't exist in a universe that is purely material. Remember, a contradiction isn't a physical thing comprised of molecules; it is a violation of a law that governs the relationship between two propositions.

Neil: I get it, Drew; you've made your point. But I'm still not buying it. I just think you are asking me to take too much on faith.

Drew: Christianity is a call to live by faith, and you are absolutely right in identifying that truth. There is a verse in the Bible, it's found in Hebrews 11:6, and it says, *"And without faith it is impossible to please Him, for whoever would draw near to God must believe that He exists and that He rewards those who seek Him."* You know, Neil, one of the things that I appreciate about our friendship is how we can talk honestly with each other and how we both enjoy a good debate. But this isn't about which of us wins a debate. I care about you and I know that

	someday you will stand before a holy God. I want you to be ready.
Neil:	I know you mean that, Drew, and I appreciate our friendship, too. But I have to be honest with you; as much as I respect your commitment to your faith, you haven't persuaded me.
Drew:	You are also a man of faith, Neil, and when I consider all the things you have to give up in order to maintain that there is no God, I have to admit that I don't have enough faith to be an atheist.
Neil:	Very funny.

~ ~ ~ ~ ~

We will leave Drew and Neil for now. In their next conversation, they will deal more directly with the question of rights and how the gospel of Jesus Christ can be expressed in terms of rights (Chapter Twelve: "Two Friends Talk Some More").

For our present purposes, we will note that Drew was asking Neil to justify his use of concepts or presuppositions that make no sense in a strictly material universe. Drew was trying to get Neil to see that he was "borrowing capital" from the Christian worldview. If they had more time, Drew would have further explained how Neil's thinking reflects what Romans 1:18-21 says about how people suppress what they know about God and the universe He created. This dialog also reflects what Romans 2:14-15 says about God's moral law being written on the human heart, including the hearts of people who have never been exposed to the written law as found in Scripture. Some Christians might think that Drew should dispense with all the reasoning and dialog and simply proclaim the gospel to Neil. After all, Romans 1:16 says,

For I am not ashamed of the gospel, for it is the power of God for salvation to everyone who believes, to the Jew first and also to the Greek.

Doesn't Drew's reliance upon human reason and argumentation get in the way of the power that is found in the gospel itself?

I am all in favor of proclaiming the gospel. According to Scripture, it is the Holy Spirit who prepares the human heart to believe and receive the gospel. If we encounter someone whose heart has already been made tender, then the need for apologetics is diminished. We need to remember, however, what was discussed in Chapter One about contemporary American culture being more like Athens than Jerusalem. A person like Neil lacks the frame of reference to connect immediately with the content of the gospel. Drew's conversation with Neil resembles Paul's message in Athens as found in Acts 17:16-30. It was not until verse 31 that Paul made direct reference to Christ.

"... because He has fixed a day on which He will judge the world in righteousness by a man whom He has appointed; and of this He has given assurance to all by raising Him from the dead."

Concerning the charge that Drew is relying on his reasoning abilities, two things should be noted. First of all, Drew's reasoning is simply a reflection of biblical truth. Although he was not constantly quoting Scripture, Drew's words were still designed to integrate biblical truth into normal conversation. Second, according to Acts 17:2, 17:17, 18:4, 19, Paul "reasoned" with people as he shared the gospel. Interestingly, the Greek word here is *dialegomai*, which means "to reason, discuss or dialog." Drew's commitment to sharing the gospel with Neil and his use of human rights to build a bridge to the gospel will be explored in Chapter Twelve: "Two Friends Talk Some More."

Chapter Eight:

Secular Dreams And Nightmares

On April 20, 1999, Columbine High School seniors Eric Harris and Dylan Klebold entered their school and began shooting and killing their classmates. Harris and Klebold murdered thirteen students and injured twenty-four more before taking their own lives.[74] In the aftermath of this horrible crime, it was reported that Harris had been wearing a t-shirt with the words NATURAL SELECTION printed on it. How much better things would have been for those victims and their families if only Harris and Klebold had subscribed to the following beliefs:

> We are concerned for the welfare of the aged,
>
> the infirm, the disadvantaged, and also

---

74   I do not make this reference to Columbine lightly. What happened there, and the lasting impact it has had on the families and friends of the victims and the survivors, must be treated with great seriousness. It is because of the seriousness of human rights that I utilize this sobering illustration.

for the outcasts – the mentally retarded, abandoned, or abused children ... These are the times for men and women of good will to further the building of a peaceful and prosperous world ... We urge recognition of the common humanity of all people. We further urge the use of reason and compassion to produce the kind of world we want – a world in which peace, prosperity, freedom, and happiness are widely shared. Let us not abandon that vision in despair or cowardice ... Let us call for an end to terror and hatred.

What is the source of this praiseworthy ethical vision? Is it the mission statement of a Christian charitable organization? Was it written by Christians trying to live the Golden Rule, "Do unto others as you would have them do to you"? The source of these admirable words is a 1973 document known as *The Humanist Manifesto II* (hereafter referred to as HMII).[75]

Eric Harris and Dylan Klebold chose to disregard the right to life possessed by the students they murdered. Again, we can only wish that they had subscribed to and

75   The original *Humanist Manifesto* was published in 1933, and was signed by thirty-four American humanists, the most famous being the philosopher John Dewey. The 1973 updated version is titled *The Humanist Manifesto II,* also known as *The Second Humanist Manifesto.* It contains an introduction, seventeen principles, and a conclusion. A third version is *The Humanist Manifesto 2000: A Call for a New Planetary Humanism.* Among its more prominent signatories are Richard Leakey, Richard Dawkins, Arthur C. Clarke, Edward O. Wilson, former United States Senator Alan Cranston and the Manifesto's primary author, Paul Kurtz. Ten Nobel Laureates are also included in the list of official endorsements. See Paul Kurtz, ed. *Humanist Manifesto I and II,* Buffalo, NY: Prometheus Books, 1973.

practiced these words from HMII:

> We would safeguard, extend, and implement the principles of human freedom evolved from the Magna Carta to the Bill of Rights, the Rights of Man, and the Universal Declaration of Human Rights.
>
> (SEVENTH principle)

> We believe in the right to universal education. Everyone has a right to the cultural opportunity to fulfill his or her unique capacities and talents. The schools should foster satisfying and productive living ... The energy and idealism of the young deserve to be appropriated and channeled to constructive purposes.
>
> (ELEVENTH principle)

In light of these words, it is especially ironic that Harris and Klebold committed their crimes in their local high school, and that ten of their victims were murdered in the school library. Harris and Klebold had the power to do what they did, but they did not have the *right* to do it.

The signers of the HMII would undoubtedly join the Christian community in condemning the murderers, but is it possible that this document could unwittingly contain a justification for the crimes committed at Columbine

High School? The signers would certainly say no, there is nothing in HMII that could justify what was done in Columbine.[76] But this denial would not be consistent with the unpleasant implications of secularism. The intention of HMII is to set aside all religious beliefs in order to construct a value system and vision for the future that leaves God out of the equation. In seeking to promote its particular secular dream, HMII sows the seeds of a secular nightmare.

Consider the following excerpts from HMII.[77]

"We find insufficient evidence for belief in the existence of a supernatural; it is either meaningless or irrelevant to the question of survival and fulfillment of the human race"

(FIRST principle)

But we can discover no divine purpose or providence for the human species.

(FIRST principle)

Modern science discredits such historic concepts as the "ghost in the machine" and

---

76   This type of charge has been leveled against the Bible by humanists many times. It is said that the Bible can be used to justify all sorts of atrocities. The test of both the Bible and HMII is whether atrocities that could be committed in their name would be consistent with the logical application of their core principles. The misuse of the Bible or HMII should not count against them. My contention is that HMII's promotion of moral relativism and its denial of universal moral absolutes unwittingly grants permission for the Eric Harrises and Dylan Klebolds of this world to do exactly what they want to do. That contention is the focus of this chapter.

77   HMII and its companion documents are fairly short and they are easily accessible on the Internet. The reader is encouraged to read them in their entirety, to see the context surrounding the specific statements I am citing in this chapter.

the "separable soul." Rather, science affirms that the human species is an emergence from natural evolutionary forces. As far as we know, the total personality is a function of the biological organism transacting in a social and cultural context.

(SECOND principle)

We affirm that moral values derive their source from human experience. Ethics is autonomous and situational needing no theological or ideological sanction. Ethics stems from human need and interest.

(THIRD principle)

We believe in maximum individual autonomy consonant with social responsibility. Although science can account for the causes of behavior, the possibilities of individual freedom of choice exist in human life and should be increased.

(FIFTH principle)

The proponents of HMII and similar documents have the best of intentions.[78] They honestly want a world in which human rights are respected and people cooperate in such a way that the maximum good is experienced by the maximum number of people. It is a good dream. What they cannot provide, however, is a compelling reason why

---

78   This compliment must be tempered by the fact that there is an underlying rebellion against God at work in HMII.

someone else has any genuine moral obligation to subscribe to it. Indeed, if the principles just cited are true, an individual or group would be free to do the exact opposite of what is proposed in HMII. Consider this dream:

> I had motives for not wanting the world to have a meaning; consequently assumed that it had none, and was able without any difficulty to find satisfying reasons for this assumption. The philosopher who finds no meaning in the world is not concerned exclusively with a problem in pure metaphysics; he is also concerned to prove that there is no valid reason why he personally should not do as he wants to do, or why his friends should not seize political power and govern in the way that they find most advantageous to themselves ... For myself, the philosophy of meaninglessness was essentially an instrument of liberation, sexual and political.
>
> (Aldous Huxley, *Ends and Means*)[79]

As part of his rejection of God, Huxley explored various forms of mysticism and experimented with hallucinogenic drugs. As he lay on his deathbed on November 22, 1963, Huxley instructed his wife to give him a large dose of LSD. Huxley's response to a universe without God is consistent with the view of man previously cited in HMII. After all, if there is no divine purpose for

79 Michael Green, *Runaway World* (Downers Grove, Illinois: Inter-Varsity Press, 1968), p. 36.

man, then we can be totally purposeless or create our own purpose, even if that purpose is to harm the people we dislike. Although Huxley was a pacifist, he saw the options that were available to others.

HMII also tells us that the sum total of the human personality is reducible to the physical processes of a brain which has evolved from a material universe as the result of chance. The personality and the moral values it chooses are nothing more than a biological organism transacting in a social and cultural context. Consequently, morality is manmade and relative to however the human personality perceives its needs and interests. This is how natural selection has programmed us to operate. If an angry and narcissistic teenager dresses in a t-shirt that says NATURAL SELECTION, carries a gun into school and begins shooting people, has he done something that is truly wrong? His actions might be disliked by others, but if he commits suicide, no one will be able to hold him accountable. What some might call a nightmare, he calls the fulfillment of a dream.

Let it again be stated that the vast majority of humanists, secularists and atheists would unreservedly condemn the actions of Harris and Klebold and they would grieve for the victims and their families. If asked to lend a hand of support, they would be first in line to help in any way they could. The signers of HMII were being honest when they professed a desire to build a world where humans would help one another and respect basic human rights. Unfortunately, they have embraced a worldview which cannot justify their secular dream without simultaneously granting Eric Harris and Dylan Klebold the philosophical and moral grounds for choosing a very different dream.

In Chapter Six: "Yes, God Exists," we considered Dr. Greg Bahnsen's critique of worldviews and the presuppositions upon which they stand:

> We can examine a worldview and ask whether its portrayal of nature, man, knowledge, etc., provide an outlook in terms of which logic, science and ethics can make sense. It does not comport with the practices of natural science to believe that all events are random and unpredictable, for instance. It does not comport with the demand for honesty in scientific research, if no moral principle expresses anything but a personal preference or feeling. Moreover, if there are internal contradictions in a person's worldview, it does not provide the preconditions for making sense out of man's experience. For instance, if one's political dogmas respect the dignity of men to make their choices, while one's psychological theories reject the free will of men, then there is an internal defect in that person's worldview.[80]

When we examine the ways in which HMII portrays morality as relative and consider that the human

---

80 Bahnsen, *Always Ready*, p. 121.

personality reduces to the scientifically measurable processes of a brain which has evolved by chance in a purely material universe lacking design or purpose, what does logical consistency demand of us? We must either allow that Eric Harris and Dylan Klebold did nothing which was absolutely and objectively wrong, that they simply did what brought them pleasure according to their own subjective standards, or we must insist that there are objective universal moral standards and universal human rights that they violated. There is nothing within HMII that would justify the belief in objective universal human rights. You cannot do away with objective moral absolutes and still retain objective universal human rights. In order to be consistent with the presuppositions of HMII, we must conclude that what Harris and Klebold did was a violation of human law as it is currently written and practiced and that their actions were unpopular. Beyond that, there would be no genuine grounds for criticizing them. They chose to do what brought them pleasure. Who are we to blame them?

Does this conclusion seem extreme? Of course it does, because the human heart knows there is a higher law which was grievously violated and that the murdered students possessed a right to life, the origin of which transcends man-made law. This stems from what we have already seen in Romans 2:14-15.

> *For when Gentiles, who do not have the law,*
> *by nature do what the law requires, they are*
> *a law to themselves, even though they do not*
> *have the law. They show that the work of the*

law is written on their hearts, while their
conscience also bears witness, and their
conflicting thoughts accuse or even excuse
them.

The Christian view says that people bear the image of God and that life did not result from a cosmic accident. There is a God who created man and endowed him with the inherent right to life. There are objective moral standards that are absolute and universal. They apply to everyone, including Eric Harris and Dylan Klebold. We know it, and deep inside their hearts, Harris and Klebold knew it, too.

The secular view espoused by HMII denies that man bears the image of God. There can be no inherent universal rights, because that would require objective morality. Man exists as the result of an unplanned natural process and his personality is a function of a biological organism controlled by the laws of chemistry and physics interacting in a social context. In other words, man is what he is because of natural selection.

These two views of humanity cannot be reconciled with each other, and this includes their opposing views of the foundations for human rights. The following dialog will invite two men to speak to us from the past. They were both brilliant spokesmen for their respective worldviews and their own words will demonstrate the irreconcilable differences on human rights that exist between Christianity and secularism or atheism. The first man is King David of the Old Testament (approximately 1040 – 970 B.C.). The second man is British mathematician and philosopher Bertrand Russell (1872-1970). David was a man after God's own heart (I Samuel 13:14). Bertrand Russell was an atheist. Their dialog is drawn from David's Psalm 139 and Russell's *A Free Man's Worship*.[81] I have used bold type wherever their works are being directly quoted.

David: Bertrand, we disagree about many things, and I am grieved by the fact that you will not honor the God who has given you life. I believe that your unbelief is a great moral wrong. I owe it to you to tell you that in plain terms. Having said that, I also want to commend you for your insight into the true nature of life in a universe without God.

Bertrand: David, you see purpose where there is none. Such wishful thinking has an emotional appeal, I recognize that. But to embrace an illusion robs you of the ability to build upon a foundation rooted in reality. **That man is the product of causes that had no prevision of the end they were achieving, that his origin, his growth, his hopes and fears, his loves, and his beliefs are but the outcome of accidental collocations of atoms, that no fire, no heroism, no intensity of thought and feeling can preserve an individual life**

81 Bertrand Russell, *Why I Am Not a Christian: And Other Essays on Religion and Related Subjects*, edited by Paul Edward, (New York: Simon and Schuster, 1957), pp. 107-116.

beyond the grave. But all the labors of the ages, all the devotion, all the inspirations, all the noon-day brightness of human genius are destined to extinction in the vast death of the solar system, and the whole temple of man's achievements must inevitably be buried beneath the debris of a universe in ruins. All these things, if not quite beyond dispute, are yet so nearly certain that no philosophy which rejects them can hope to stand. Only within the scaffolding of these truths, only on the firm foundation of unyielding despair can the soul's habitation henceforth be safely built.

David: Truer words have never been spoken. If there is no God, then unyielding despair is the soul's habitation. Nothing we strive for, nothing we build, no relationship with a loved one will matter when we die. The grave equals our complete extinction. But, thankfully, the universe is much different than how you describe it, Bertrand. And, yes, there is a referent for my thankfulness. When I consider my place in this universe, I find myself praying, **O LORD, you have searched me and known me! You know when I sit down and when I rise up; you discern my thoughts from afar. You search out my path and my lying down and are acquainted with all my ways. Even** before a word is on my tongue, behold, O LORD, you know it altogether. You hem me in, behind and before, and lay your hand upon me. Such knowledge is too wonderful for me; it is high; I cannot attain it. Where shall I go from your Spirit? Or where shall I flee from your presence? If I ascend to heaven, you are there! If I make my bed in Sheol, you are there! If I take the wings of the morning and dwell in the uttermost parts of the sea, even there your hand shall lead me, and your right hand shall hold me.

Bertrand: Those are beautiful words, David. Your skills as a poet are admirable. But there is no one out there to hear your prayers. You are retreating from reality. I choose to face it. **Brief and powerless is man's life, on him and all his race the slow sure doom falls pitiless and dark. Blind good and evil, wreckless of destruction, omnipotent matter rolls on its relentless way. For man condemned today to lose his dearest, tomorrow himself to pass through the gate of darkness. It remains only to cherish, ere yet the blow falls, the lofty thoughts that ennoble his little day. Proudly defiant of the irresistible forces that tolerate, for a moment, his knowledge and his condemnation, to sustain alone a weary but unyielding atlas, the world that**

his own ideals have fashioned despite the trampling march of unconscious power. This is the universe in which we live.

David: It is you who have chosen the path of delusion Bertrand. I choose praise precisely because of how God has made the universe. O LORD, **you formed my inward parts; you knitted me together in my mother's womb. I praise you, for I am fearfully and wonderfully made. Wonderful are your works; my soul knows it very well. My frame was not hidden from you, when I was being made in secret, intricately woven in the depths of the earth. Your eyes saw my unformed substance; in your book were written, every one of them, the days that were formed for me, when as yet there was none of them. How precious to me are your thoughts, O God! How vast is the sum of them! If I would count them, they are more than the sand. I awake, and I am still with you.** Bertrand, you describe your worldview as "a free man's worship." You have told me that man is the product of causes that had no prevision of the end they were achieving, that his origin, his growth, his hopes and fears, his love, and his beliefs are but the outcome of accidental collocations (arrangement) of atoms. Bertrand, don't you see that if the universe is what you say it is, then it is wishful thinking to talk about freedom?

Bertrand: But I *am* free, David. The choices I make, I make for myself, not for some God who tells me I should live in fear of him.

David: You have no freedom. Freedom is an illusion; it does not correspond to reality. For, as you yourself have proclaimed, "Brief and powerless is man's life, on him and all his race the slow sure doom falls pitiless and dark. Blind good and evil, wreckless of destruction, omnipotent matter rolls on its relentless way." Bertrand, in your universe, you make no choices. The accidental collocations of atoms that have no prevision of the ends they are achieving make your choices for you. Even your beliefs are controlled by the accidental collocations of atoms. To be consistent within your worldview, you must abandon any real basis for the human rights that the people of your era claim to possess and that you have argued for.

Bertrand: Then perhaps **only within the scaffolding of these truths, only on the firm foundation of unyielding despair can the soul's habitation be safely built**. And, David, I find this to be far preferable than a life of fear.

David: The LORD is my shepherd. I fear no evil.

Bertrand: David, neither one of us will persuade the other, but our deaths will resolve the differences in our views.

David: Yes, Bertrand, in that regard you are certainly
          correct.

~ ~ ~ ~ ~

We will leave Bertrand Russell and David at this point. Bertrand Russell would have been just as appalled by the actions of Eric Harris and Dylan Klebold as the humanists who subscribe to HMII. Yet, according to the worldview represented in *A Free Man's Worship*, Russell's moral beliefs originated from an accidental collocation of atoms, as did the moral beliefs of Harris and Klebold. In this worldview, everyone's moral beliefs are purely subjective. There are no objective standards that exist independently of man. Consequently, human rights can have no objective existence, either. Since everything reduces to the subjectivity of the individual, why should one individual have to respect the rights of another individual?

The best answer that a secularist can come up with to respect human rights in an atheist universe is to appeal to utilitarianism. This is a system that defines right as being that which promotes the greatest good for the greatest number. That sounds fine until you find yourself in a minority. If it benefits two people to deprive one person of his life or his property, isn't that a greater good than letting one person survive? The problem with utilitarianism is that it requires a system of calculation that is impossible to know. The utilitarianism of a secularist will always reduce to subjectivism and the will of the majority (or the most powerful minority) being imposed on everyone else.

The Christian worldview is perfectly consistent with its core presuppositions. There is a God who created us and has endowed us with universal objective human rights. Because God Himself is the source of those rights, their existence does not depend on the subjective preferences of individual people or human governments. Included with objective human rights are objective moral standards that we are all obligated to obey. They are absolute and universal. There are not exemptions for individuals like Eric Harris and Dylan Klebold who choose to act as though "ethics is autonomous and situational, needing no theological sanction." Unlike HMII, Christianity understands that there is an afterlife and a time of judgment when people will be held accountable for their actions. Killing yourself after murdering thirteen students will not insulate you from accountability and justice.

When it comes to human rights, the paths of Christianity and secularism or atheism lead in opposite directions. Either God is the measure of all things or man is. The writer of Proverbs saw this clearly when he wrote:

There is a way that seems right to a man,
but its end is the way to death.

Proverbs 14:12

God is the source of human rights and of all the human rights that a person can possess, one stands out above all the rest. This wonderful right is offered freely to all who will receive it by faith alone:

> *But to all who did receive Him, who believed in His name, He gave the right to become children of God.*

John 1:12

This is the Christian response to America's debate about rights.

Chapter Nine:

Getting Rights Right

This book is about rights, how rights fit into the Christian worldview and how Christians can and must engage the culture in the arena of rights. From the outset, we have noted that America is the most rights-conscious society in history. It seems as though almost every moral or political issue of the day is eventually framed in terms of rights. Because people are so prone to take rights seriously, Christians have an opportunity to present the gospel of Jesus Christ by using the common ground of rights-talk as a point of contact with their non-Christian neighbors. Included in this process can be a defense or apologetic for the Christian worldview in general and for a Christian view of rights in particular.

However, there does seem to be a major drawback to using rights to explain the gospel and to defend the Christian worldview. Are we not simultaneously opening the door to great controversy which can detract from the gospel and invite persecution? One need look no further than to the gay rights/gay marriage movement to see how intensely the issue of rights is being debated in America. Is it wise to use this forum for sharing the gospel? My answer to that question is that not only is it wise, but it also must become a top priority for the church in America.[82] We must get rights right!

There is a well-known figure of speech that talks about "the elephant in the room." That is an imaginative way of describing the existence of a situation so obvious that it merits discussion. However, for reasons of embarrassment or a desire to avoid controversy, people avoid discussing the situation. It is akin to a group of people gathered in a living room that has an elephant standing in the middle of it. They talk about many things, but no one brings up the presence of the elephant. The fact that no one mentions the elephant does not mean they aren't thinking about it, however. Many people reading this book have perhaps been wondering if and when the issue of gay rights would be brought up. Gay rights are not the exclusive topic of this present chapter, but they will be included. This chapter will present a basic explanation for how rights should function in a society and how we should understand the existence of rights not specifically acknowledged in the Bible. While we should not seek to create controversy, there are times when taking truth seriously makes controversy unavoidable. When it comes

---

82   My use of *church* in this context refers to the congregations and the denominations that hold the inspiration, infallibility and authority of Scripture in high regard. These are churches that are unwilling to accommodate changing cultural moral norms, if those norms directly contradict clear scriptural standards historically held by the church.

to rights in America, there is an elephant in the room whose presence cannot be ignored.

This book has been critical of the view that says rights do not depend upon God and that no transcendent foundation for rights exists or is needed.[83] If a transcendent foundation is rejected, then all that remains for protecting or establishing rights is a political process that, while having a veneer of civility and benevolence, is little more than the will of the political class imposed upon those who lack the power to oppose them.

Is a transcendent foundation necessary for rights to exist? As I write these words, I am in possession of a driver's license for the State of Ohio. This license gives me the legal right to drive a car on the roads of Ohio. All other states recognize the validity of this license, so I am granted the legal right to drive on their roads as well. Doesn't the existence of this right demonstrate that human law is all that is necessary for a right to exist? After all, there is no verse in the Bible that addresses the issue of driver's licenses and the right to drive a car, but I do believe I possess that right.

There is a sense in which we can create rights by enacting new laws. In 1880, there were no automobiles in Ohio and no driver's licenses. The right to drive a car did not exist then, but it does exist now. That is because Ohio, along with the other states, has passed laws which

---

83   Keep in mind that the word "transcendent" as used in this context speaks of that which is above or beyond a particular realm or sphere. To deny that there is a transcendent foundation for rights is to say that there is nothing greater than or beyond man-made law or politics that accounts for the existence of rights.

created that right.[84] The existence of the right to drive does not seem to require a transcendent or supernatural foundation.

A similar example can be seen in woman's suffrage (the right to vote). The Nineteenth Amendment to the Constitution of the United States, which was adopted in 1920, reads as follows:

> The right of citizens of the United States to vote shall not be denied or abridged by the United States or by any state on account of sex.
>
> (Amendment 19, Clause 1)

Although some of the Western states were already permitting women to vote, it was the Nineteenth Amendment that gave women in all parts of the United States the right to vote in state and national elections. This is a right that I am very glad to see my wife and age-eligible daughters exercise. I openly admit that I exercise my right to drive in Ohio and my wife exercises her right to vote in Ohio, and that I believe such rights exist even though there is no mention of them in the Bible. Doesn't this admission contradict my central thesis that rights depend upon God?

The Christian worldview is not opposed to the existence of legal rights which have no direct mention in Scripture, such as the right to drive a car or to vote in an election. By legal rights, we mean a right that is directly created by the enacting of a law. In this sense, they are

---

84   For the purpose of this illustration, there is no need to provide a historical survey of the origins of the legislation that created driver's licenses.

different than objective universal human rights such as the right to life, a right with which we are endowed by God and that does not depend on a human law for its existence. Legal rights can be a great blessing within a society, and as a society changes and evolves, new legal rights can be created and older ones can be eliminated. Had I lived in Ohio in 1880, I would have had certain rights pertaining to riding a horse down the middle of Main Street. It is no longer appropriate for me to have that legal right in a major city and I don't believe I have suffered an injustice in having that legal right taken away by law.[85]

It would be a mistake, however, to think that legal rights created by human law do not need a transcendent foundation. The Bible explains how a legal right can have a transcendent foundation, even if it is not mentioned in the Bible and is not a universal human right. According to Romans 13:1-7, the institution of human government is sanctioned by God and is granted authority over the individual by God:

> *Let every person be subject to the governing*
> *authorities. For there is no authority except*
> *from God, and those that exist have been*
> *instituted by God.*
> Romans 13:1

This passage in no way grants governments operated by humans carte blanche (unrestricted authority) to do whatever they please without restraint,

---

85 Exceptions which a community might make for Amish or Mennonites who use horse-drawn carriages are beside the point for the purpose of this illustration.

but for our present purposes, we are observing that these governments are sanctioned by God. God recognizes that I have a right to drive a car in Ohio, because the government of Ohio has issued me a license to that effect. My wife has a right to vote in Ohio given to her by the Nineteenth Amendment of the Constitution of the United States. Our entitlement to these rights is not directly based upon being created in God's image and the rights are not inalienable,[86] which means they can be rightfully taken away under circumstances written into the law. If I commit a series of drunk driving violations, I can lose my license, which would not be a violation of my rights. In other words, being created in the image of God does not automatically give me the right to drive.

According to the Bible, human government exists because God has ordained government as a practical means for providing order and security within a community or nation. When a government creates a legitimate legal right, whether by statute, constitutional provision or case law, it is functioning in accordance with God's purpose and will. A legal right can grant me a privilege such as driving a car on public roads and it can grant me a protection. When the government punishes an unlicensed driver or revokes the license of an unsafe driver, there is an implicit recognition that the public has the right to expect that the roadways will be kept reasonably safe. Both the privileges and the protections of legal rights are sanctioned by God.

For rulers are not a terror to good conduct,
but to bad. Would you have no fear of the one

---

86 An *inalienable* right refers to a right that is not transferable and cannot be taken away.

who is in authority? Then do what is good,
and you will receive his approval, for he is
God's servant for your good. But if you do
wrong, be afraid, for he does not bear the
sword in vain. For he is the servant of God,
an avenger who carries out God's wrath on
the wrongdoer.

Romans 13:3-4

According to the Christian worldview, even legal rights have a transcendent foundation. This doesn't ignore the fact that, unlike universal human rights, legal rights are relative to specific cultures and governments and can change over time.

It should also be noted that Paul's words in Romans 13:3-4 were written during the time of the Roman Empire. Obviously, the Roman government had no sense that they were serving the Christian God and, had they been informed of that truth, they would have denied it. People have been forming societies and governments since very early in human history, without being consciously aware that God Himself has ordained this activity. I believe it is one of the chief manifestations of God's common grace as described in Chapter Four: "And God Said, "Let There Be Rights." God's common grace does not need to be perceived or understood in order for it to operate within human societies.

Another aspect of the Christian view of government is that no government has absolute authority and therefore not everything a government might do (including creating a particular legal right) is legitimate or binding. A compelling example of this principle is found in Acts 5. In the earliest days of Christianity when the gospel was still largely confined to Jerusalem, the apostles were busy proclaiming the resurrection of Jesus Christ. This was very distressing to the Sanhedrin, which was the ruling body over Israel. The Sanhedrin had engineered the arrest, trial and execution of Jesus on charges of blasphemy. If Jesus had subsequently risen from the dead, then the obvious conclusion would have been that the rulers had committed a great sin and that they had murdered Israel's long-awaited Messiah. The Sanhedrin invoked its governing authority by threatening the apostles and ordering them to stop preaching the Christian gospel:

> *And when they had brought them, they set them before the council. And the high priest questioned them saying, "We strictly charged you not to teach in this name, yet here you have filled Jerusalem with your teaching, and you intend to bring this man's blood upon us." But Peter and the apostles answered, "We must obey God rather than men."*

Acts 5:27-29

Peter and the other apostles were not anti-authoritarian agitators. Under normal circumstances, they would have held the authority of the Sanhedrin in high regard, in keeping with the theology later written into Romans 13:1-7. But Peter understood that when any human government exercises its authority in a manner which is directly contrary to God's authority, government can be opposed (at least in the specific area where that government is in rebellion against God's law).[87]

Within the Christian worldview, it is possible to say that a right can exist and not exist at the same time.[88] I believe gay marriage is one such right. In order to justify this claim I would point to what the Bible teaches about idols. Isaiah 44-47 contains an extended discussion about idols and idolatry. The people of Israel had corrupted themselves by imitating the beliefs and practices of the pagan nations which surrounded them. God, speaking through the prophet Isaiah, exposed the stupidity of worshipping an idol. In Isaiah 44:9-20, there is a sarcastic description of the craftsman who fashions an idol out of wood. This man carefully selects the tree that will provide wood for his idol. He cuts it down,

> *Then it becomes fuel for a man. He takes a part of it and warms himself; he kindles a fire and bakes bread. Also he makes a god and worships it; he makes it an idol and falls down before it. Half of it he burns in the fire. Over the half he eats meat; he roasts it and is satisfied ... And the rest of it he makes into a god, his idol, and falls down to it and worships it.*

> Isaiah 44:15-17A

---

87   This is a fallen world where sin is present. No human government will ever be perfect and Acts 5:29 should not be used as an excuse to undermine or overthrow a government the moment it does something which is contrary to Scripture. In some ways, the Roman Empire was very ungodly, but Romans 13:1-7 was written in that environment. It is interesting to note that the Declaration of Independence went to great lengths to document "a long train of abuses and usurpations" by King George III as evidence that the Declaration was drafted only as a last resort.

88   An explanation will be given as to why this statement does not violate the law of contradiction.

In the midst of this portrayal of idols and idolatry, God repeatedly declares that He alone is God:

I am the LORD, and there is no other, beside
me there is no God;

Isaiah 45:5

Idols and idolatry were a very real phenomenon (and still are). The people of God, in both the Old and New Testaments, are warned to avoid idols (see I John 5:21). Idols exist and people who worship them are deceived. There is another sense, however, in which idols do not exist. In the Isaiah 44 passage just cited, it is as though God was saying of the man's handiwork, "It is just a chunk of wood and will never be anything more than a chunk of wood. The god represented by that wood is not real, it does not exist."[89]

The Apostle Paul also taught this dual reality in I Corinthians 8. The city of Corinth was famous for its idols and idolatry. The Corinthians who converted to Christianity not only had to give up their former idolatry, but they also had to stop thinking through the lens of an idolatrous worldview. Note what Paul wrote about idols:

Therefore, as to the eating of food offered
to idols, we know that "an idol has no real
existence" and that "there is no God but one".

I Corinthians 8:4

On the immediate temporal level, idols did exist in Corinth. They were abundant and plain to see throughout

---

89 The piece of wood fashioned into an idol was intended to be a point of contact with the god it represented. But as is often the case with idolatry, the physical objects can themselves become objects of worship, as though the objects possess some supernatural property.

the city. Paul granted that as an obvious state of affairs. But Paul recognized that there is another realm, what we might call an ultimate reality, a transcendent reality or a spiritual reality. Like the present material world in which we live, this ultimate reality depends upon God and His truth. It is in this ultimate reality that, according to I Corinthians 8:4, "an idol has no real existence." I would suggest the following as an amplified paraphrase of I Corinthians 8:4:

> *Therefore, as to the eating of food offered to idols, we know that the wood or stone statue that people worship as their god is nothing more than a hunk of wood or chunk of stone and that is all it will ever be. What it is supposed to represent, some god or goddess worshipped by the people of Corinth, isn't real - it doesn't exist. It is the fantasy of a sinful human mind which is deluded and deceived. It doesn't correspond to reality.*

Using this biblical truth, I would state that a legal right can exist and not exist at the same time. In other words, a legal right can exist in a law code, but if God doesn't acknowledge that legal or political right as being genuine or legitimate then it does not truly exist where it matters most, the courtroom of a holy God. If a law were passed which entitled people with brown eyes to confiscate all the property of blue-eyed people once every five years, a brown-eyed person could say that he has a legal right to that property. But come judgment day, when that person stands before the righteous Judge of the universe, he will be guilty of having broken the commandment, "You shall not steal." Given the opportunity, the brown eyed person might say, "But God, I had the legal right to take that property, so it doesn't count as stealing." That legal right is in the same category as the idol in I Corinthians 8:4.

Therefore, as to the eating of food offered to idols, we know that "an idol has no real existence" and that "there is no God but one".

In the case of the brown-eyed person, his legal right exists on a piece of paper crafted by human legislation. He can hold that piece of paper in his hand and say, "Look, it is written here, I have the legal right to take that property." That paper does exist, the printed words do say that he has a legal right to that property and his local court will uphold his actions. However, there is a higher law (it is not man-made) that says, "You shall not steal." No human legislation, case law or constitutional provision can legitimately create a legal right if that legal right directly contradicts God's moral law.

The Christian worldview teaches that there is an ultimate Supreme Court and God is the Judge:

And I saw the dead, great and small, standing before the throne, and books were opened. Then another book was opened, which is the book of life. And the dead were judged by what was written in the books, according to what they had done.

Revelation 20:12

Whatever legal rights a person may possess in this life will not serve as a legitimate excuse before God if the exercise of that legal right violated God's moral law. A similar principle was applied to Nazi criminals after World War II in the Nuremberg Trials.[90] Although its theological implications were not explored, an appeal was made to a concept called "crimes against humanity." Just because something might be legal does not mean it is morally innocent.

While a person will ultimately be judged for his obedience or disobedience to God's moral law, there is a sense in which this judgment evaluates whether or not legitimate human law was obeyed. This goes back to the biblical command to obey duly established human authority, which appears in Romans 13:1-7. If the speed limit on the interstate is 65 miles per hour, then I am sinning if I drive at 90 miles per hour. This particular human law was duly established by the government and since it does not violate the higher law (God's moral law), it is to be obeyed.[91] Obedience to laws we dislike, and respect for the legal rights of others, including those rights we disagree with, is essential to the maintenance of society. Of all people, Christians should be law-abiding and do everything possible to promote peace and civility.

---

90   The legal and moral issues brought up during the Nuremberg Trials are too complex to adequately address in this book. I am simply drawing attention to the fact that even in human courts there is precedent for saying that what is a legal right within a particular society's legal code can be condemned as criminal by appealing to a broader standard. I also acknowledge that an argument can be made that what happened at the Nuremberg Trials was simply a matter of "victor's justice."

91   On a personal note, I dislike seatbelt laws and believe that such laws, no matter how well-intentioned, are too much of an intrusion upon individual liberty. However, as a Christian, I acknowledge my duty to obey that law and, if I feel strongly enough about it, use the legal process to win a repeal of that law. Personally, I do not feel strongly enough about it to engage the legal process, so I wear my seatbelt.

First of all, then, I urge that supplications,
prayers, intercessions, and thanksgivings be
made for all people, for kings and all who
are in high positions, that we may lead a
peaceful and quiet life, godly and dignified
in every way.

I Timothy 2:1-2

What happens when a Christian's duty to obey
God's law puts him or her at odds with human authority?
When the Sanhedrin ordered Peter and the apostles to stop
preaching the gospel, Peter replied that he was obligated
to submit to the higher authority of God: *"We must obey
God rather than men"* (Acts 5:29). Peter took no delight
in defying the Sanhedrin, but he understood where his
highest duty was. Because America is simultaneously a
rights-conscious society and has largely embraced moral
relativism, Christians need to understand how to properly
balance their obligation to submit to human authority with
their higher obligation to God. Perhaps most importantly,
Christians need to see the opportunities to share the gospel
that exist precisely because of the controversial nature of
various rights claims.

The following conversation takes place between
Kirsten (Christian) and Michelle (non-Christian), the two
women we met in Chapter Two: "Speaking of Rights." This
time, they are talking about gay marriage and Kirsten's
church. Obviously, this is a controversial and politically
charged topic, but in keeping with the main theme of this
book, Kirsten wants to share the gospel and defend the

Christian worldview. While this will inevitably intersect with political matters, Kirsten's primary concern is not politics, but the spiritual needs of her friend, Michelle.

Michelle: So if a gay couple asked your church to marry them the answer would be no?

Kirsten: You're right, the answer would be no. My pastor would not participate in performing a gay marriage ceremony.

Michelle: I can't believe how intolerant that is! The sooner homophobia disappears, the better. Not only is your church unloving, it is probably breaking anti-discrimination laws. A gay couple has the same rights that you have and it is very hateful of your pastor not to respect their rights.

Kirsten: Michelle, you just put about five big issues on the table and you've made some strong accusations. I'd like to respond, if you would be interested in hearing an answer.

Michelle: If you want to try to defend the indefensible, go ahead.

Kirsten: Well, the first thing I want to mention is something that I won't spend much time on, even though it's important. You accused my church of being intolerant, right?

Michelle: I sure did.

Kirsten: And you know something Michelle? You're absolutely right, we are intolerant, and that's why you should join us, because you're intolerant, too.

Michelle: How can you say that?

Kirsten: Michelle, when I explained my church's moral beliefs to you, you were outraged. If you had your way, our beliefs would be done away with. Don't you see that certain things strike you as being intolerable? I have found that people who pride themselves on being open-minded and tolerant stand ready to condemn people they see as being close-minded and intolerant. The bottom line is everyone has things they don't tolerate and things they close their minds to. The last time we talked, you made it clear that you would not tolerate a law that gave men the legal right to rape a woman who wears jeans in public. Doesn't your non-compliant attitude make you intolerant?

Michelle: That's different, and you know it.

Kirsten: Why is your intolerance acceptable but somebody else's intolerance is not acceptable? Michelle, I obviously agree with you about not tolerating the legal right to rape, but I'm trying to show you that intolerance, by itself, is a morally neutral thing. What makes it right or wrong is the specific thing we apply it to. That's what the debate should focus on. Just going around calling people we disagree with "intolerant," and thinking that automatically makes us right is a waste of time. Intolerance can be wrong in some instances, and right in others.

Michelle: But my problem with your church, Kirsten, is that it is unloving.

Kirsten: Why do you think that? Is it because we don't recognize gay marriage?

Michelle: I'd say that's an open and shut case. You guys hate homosexuals.

Kirsten: First of all, there have been instances where Christians have been unloving and unkind to people –

Michelle: So you admit it!

Kirsten: Yes, and take that admission as a confession of sin on our part. When a Christian shows hatred toward a fellow sinner, he or she is guilty of hypocrisy. It is very wrong, but sometimes we act as though other people's sins are worse than our own. God commands us to love everyone, and there's plenty of room for improvement in that department. But, Michelle, loving someone also includes an obligation to speak the truth about sin. This isn't to put people down; it is to alert them to their need for God's forgiveness and His power to change their lives. Sometimes we speak the truth and forget to season it with a spirit of grace and love. And sometimes, no matter how much grace and love we include, people still resent hearing God's truth and they resent those who declare it.

Michelle: Maybe the things you call sin aren't really sins at all. Maybe this is about your personal prejudices.

Kirsten: Again, guilty as charged. Michelle, Christians are vulnerable to doing that very thing – taking their own preferences and judging other people for not sharing those preferences. I've caught myself doing that to other people. Now, having admitted that, I would be willing to do a Bible study with you to let you see the testimony of Scripture. I think you will find it speaks very clearly on God's standards for marriage.

Michelle: So what if it does? Gay couples still have a right to get married.

Kirsten: Based on recent developments they do have a legal right, as far as the law gives them that right. But as you and I have discussed before, history is filled with examples of legal rights that were moral wrongs. If I had owned slaves in 1840 in Mississippi, I could have split up a family by selling part of it to another slave owner. I had that right according to the law.[92] But I don't think my actions would have met with God's approval, and so in His eyes I did not have the right to split up that family, and that's what ultimately matters.

Michelle: Why do you insist on comparing apples with oranges? I find it incredibly offensive that you would equate the right to gay marriage with something as terrible as human slavery.

Kirsten: Michelle, you and I disagree over the morality

---

92   Kirsten's example is meant to illustrate her point that having a legal right to do something doesn't shield it from moral critique. The particular regulations that actually existed in 1840 Mississippi are not the point of her illustration.

or immorality of gay marriage, at least on the surface. But as a Christian, I believe there is a higher law, a law which trumps human law if and when obeying a human law conflicts with obeying the higher law. This has been a Christian precept for 2,000 years, and it has often resulted in the persecution and even martyrdom of Christians.

Michelle: Give me a break! You're calling yourself the victim in this case?

Kirsten: No. But I am honestly telling you that I can see the day coming when the American church will pay a high price for standing on biblical truth.[93]

Michelle: So what are you going to do, start a rebellion just because society won't accept your bigotry?

Kirsten: Of course not, Michelle. What I hope will happen, if persecution comes, is that the church will be revived and Christians will do more than fill up seats in a worship service. And if that revival happens, then more Christians will be willing to tell our gay neighbors, and everyone else, about the best right imaginable, a right far more wonderful than anything human law can create. And one of the best features of this right is that no human law will ever be able to take it away. Michelle, I already possess this right, and I want you to have it, too. And if a

---

93   Again, the use of the word "church" in this context refers to the congregations and denominations that hold the inspiration, infallibility and authority of Scripture in high regard. These are churches that are unwilling to accommodate changing cultural norms, if those norms directly contradict clear scriptural standards historically held by the church.

gay couple came to our pastor and asked him to perform their wedding ceremony, I know my pastor would, in a spirit of love, tell them about a right that far surpasses a man-made legal right to gay marriage. Do you know what this right is?

Michelle: I'm not sure I understand your point.

Kirsten: Michelle, the Bible makes this promise to me, to you, and to anyone who will take it to heart. This is what it says about Jesus Christ: "He was in the world, and the world was made through Him, yet the world did not know Him. He came to His own, and His own people did not receive Him. But to all who did receive Him, who believed in His name, He gave the right to become children of God."

~ ~ ~ ~ ~

We will leave Kirsten and Michelle at this point. Their conversation about gay marriage could go in a multitude of directions and take many hours to explore. While such a discussion would be very valuable, it goes beyond the scope of this book.[94] The purpose of this dialog, and of this chapter, is to distinguish between legal rights which come from human law, constitutional provision and case law, and a higher law or transcendent

---

94   This book was not written to offer or promote a political strategy for dealing with the controversial aspects of human rights and legal rights. There is room in the Christian worldview for Christians to be politically active and I believe there is an obligation to protect the legitimate rights of the oppressed (Proverbs 31:8-9). Appropriate political activity, even when successful, will never be able to change an individual or a culture like the gospel can.

law from which universal human rights originate. When Christians understand this distinction, they will be better able to engage the culture and find creative ways to communicate the unchanging gospel of Jesus Christ to a world in desperate need of good news.

Chapter Ten:

Has God Violated Human Rights?

Many skeptics believe that the strongest case against the biblical view of human rights is found in the Bible itself. Several portions of Scripture cast God in what is, by contemporary standards, a very unflattering light. At times, God's morality seems to be decidedly immoral, and the actions He commands of others or permits them to do seem to be violations of human rights of the grossest sorts. We have already noted what Dr. Dershowitz of Harvard Law School thinks about the Bible's track record:

> "It insults God to believe that it was He who mandated eternal inequality for women, execution for gays, slavery, animal sacrifice, and the scores of immoral laws of the Bible, the Koran, and other books purported to be speaking in God's name. Humans falsely

speaking in God's name are to blame for these immoralities..."[95]

It must be remembered that Dr. Dershowitz is an atheist. It is not as though he believes in God and blames the Bible for misrepresenting who God really is. The point he is making is that in the Bible, he finds all sorts of immoral laws and mandates that are violations of what should be seen as basic human rights. The view of rights presented in The Rights Fight is based upon a belief that God exists and the Bible is His Word. The question that has been asked and needs to be answered is this: "Has God violated human rights?" If He has, then the entire Christian worldview is flawed and surrenders all credibility in the arena of human rights.

This chapter will consider three examples of God's alleged violations of human rights. They are:

    1)   God's endorsement of slavery.

    2)   His support of genocide.

    3)   His allowing of human suffering.

Consider the existence of slavery in the Bible. As God was giving His law in Exodus 21:1-11, He did not abolish slavery, He simply regulated it. Even in the New Testament, Christian slave owners were given instructions for the proper treatment of slaves (Ephesians 6:9). Nothing was said about emancipation.

There is also the problem of genocide. On more than one occasion, God ordered the people of Israel to attack other peoples and annihilate them. The descriptions found in Numbers 31 regarding the destruction of the Midianites and in I Samuel 15:1-7 regarding the destruction of the Amalekites read like modern-day war crimes.

> *Thus says the LORD of hosts, "I have noted what Amalek did to Israel in opposing them on the way when they came up out of Egypt. Now go and strike Amalek and devote to destruction all that they have. Do not spare them, but kill both man and woman, child and infant, ox and sheep, camel and donkey."*
>
> I Samuel 15:2-3

The third issue we will consider is the perplexing problem of suffering.[96] We are all familiar with the scenes on television of diseased and starving children. A tsunami strikes and thousands of children are left homeless, parentless, and alone. A grieving young mother searches among the piles of decaying bodies and has her worst fear realized when she finds her child among them. God is in control of tsunamis. It was said of Jesus Christ that the wind and the waves obey Him (Mark 4:41). Reader, if you had the power to stop that deadly tsunami, what would you have done? God has that power and He let it happen. What kind of God imposes moral duties upon others while doing nothing to save innocent people?

---

96 Suffering and evil are often categorized as being either natural evil or moral evil. Natural evil is thought of as those events in nature which cause human suffering (drought, earthquake, flood, disease). Moral evil results from the choices made by moral agents which inflict suffering on others. Murder, rape, persecution, cruelty and unjust wars are types of moral evil. The point is that whether caused by the forces of nature or by the actions of people, suffering and evil are pervasive.

Of all the arguments against Christianity and the Christian view of human rights, these are among the most persuasive. I am not saying they are sound arguments, but they are persuasive. I have no doubt that some skeptics make use of them simply to score points. But for most people it is far more personal than that. Christians often struggle with these issues as well. How could anyone witness the suffering which is so widespread and remain unmoved? As a pastor, I have made countless hundreds of hospital calls and conducted funerals under the most difficult of circumstances. I completely understand the impulse people have to ask questions such as, "Why would a loving God permit a child to be molested? Why would God permit cancer to kill a young mother? Why didn't God steer that tornado away from the town?" If these types of questions can't be given adequate answers, then there is good reason to doubt the whole foundation upon which the Christian view of human rights is built.

The classic argument against the existence of a benevolent God is the one given by the ancient Greek philosopher Epicurus (341 – 270 B.C.). Epicurus wasn't necessarily arguing for atheism the way a contemporary skeptic would define atheism. But he was claiming that the gods of ancient Greece were not benevolent (good) and were not concerned about the daily lives of the Greek people. His argument, adapted for present purposes, can be roughly stated as follows:

> If God has the knowledge and power necessary to end suffering (evil) but does not do it, then he is not benevolent. If God

has the desire and the knowledge necessary but does not end suffering then he is not all-powerful. If he has the power and desire to end suffering but does not do it, then he is not all-knowing. Suffering and evil continue to exist, therefore a loving, all-powerful, all knowing God does not exist.

In this chapter, I will provide a theodicy for God. A theodicy is a justification of the ways of God.[97] I state that with caution, because as someone who believes the Bible I know that ultimately God needs no defense. He is not on trial. I am but a lump of clay (II Corinthians 4:7), and so are God's accusers (Romans 9:19-21). Perhaps I should say that this theodicy is a defense of my belief in the God who is the author of universal human rights. It is not God who is being defended, but my belief in Him. It is difficult to write an apologetic for the Christian view of human rights, especially a theodicy, without sounding as though it is God Himself who is being defended. That is not my intention, but because of my limitations as a writer, it might seem that way.

One thing this theodicy will not do is retreat from the historic Christian teaching that God is the sovereign Ruler over this universe and that He is in control of all that happens. The Babylonian King, Nebuchadnezzar, having

---

97   The word "theodicy" comes from two words, "theos" (God) and "dikai" (righteous or just). A theodicy seeks to give a sufficient reason for the evil or suffering God permits. As such, a theodicy is a justification of the ways of God. A theodicy offered in strong terms will state the actual reason for evil. A less ambitious theodicy will only offer a possible reason, one which makes belief in God's goodness at least a rational belief, but does not claim absolute certainty. I recommend John Feinberg, *The Many Faces of Evil: Theological Systems and the Problem of Evil.* (Wheaton, Illinois: Crossway Books, 2004).

been humbled by the disciplinary hand of God, confessed:

> *...for His dominion is an everlasting dominion, and His kingdom endures from generation to generation; all the inhabitants of the earth are accounted as nothing, and He does according to His will among the host of heaven and among the inhabitants of the earth; and none can stay His hand or say to Him, "What have you done?"*
>
> Daniel 4:34b-35

Some contemporary Christian theologians have tried to deal with the problem of evil by proposing that God's knowledge of the future and His control over events is limited by the decisions people make. Under certain conditions, human decisions will be more determinative of what happens in the future than the decrees and sovereign will of God. This comes dangerously close to replacing the God of Scripture with a false god. God is omnipotent (all-powerful), omniscient (all-knowing) and benevolent (good). He has endowed all people with certain rights that reflect both His moral character and His having created us in His image.

Before addressing the Bible's treatment of slavery, genocide and suffering, there is a more basic truth that needs to be recognized. In an atheist universe, there can be no problem of evil. When an atheist points to the suffering or evil he sees and then uses it to attack God, he is borrowing capital from the Christian worldview. In the Christian worldview, it is reasonable to think that there is a standard of goodness against which other things can be measured. This standard is universal and objective. That's another way of saying that it is true everywhere, at all times, for everyone. If we use a standard of goodness that is not universal and is not objective, then what right does Person A have to judge Person B by Person A's standard? Why can't Person B (and that includes God in the role of Person B) have a different standard and, therefore, a different value system? If Person A thinks slavery is wrong, then Person A shouldn't own slaves. But why should Person B think that he has any obligation to satisfy Person A's sense of how things ought to be?

For there to be a problem of evil, evil has to exist. For the word "evil" to mean anything, it has to refer to some standard that is universally and objectively true for everyone. Did Hitler do evil? Why couldn't he simply claim that in his particular value system the purification and preservation of the Aryan race was a sufficient justification for seeking to exterminate or sterilize the people he considered to be unfit? Just because a Jew might call Hitler evil, why should Hitler have to accept another person's standard of what makes something an act of evil?

The Christian worldview takes evil seriously, because it has the necessary preconditions for evil to exist.[98] These preconditions include universal, objective morality and non-material things which have real existence such as duty, morality, justice, love, hate, right, wrong, good, evil and objective human rights. A universe which is merely matter in motion cannot justify anything being called evil

---

98   The word "exist" means "to stand out." We say that something exists when it makes a difference in our experience.

or even the very existence of evil, itself. After all, what is evil? It is not something which is material. In other words, it is not something that can be examined under a microscope like a strand of human hair. Evil is not colored blue and it does not weigh three pounds. It does not smell like coffee beans, possess a smooth texture and make high-pitched sounds. Whatever evil is, it has no material substance. Many atheists deny the existence of God or other immaterial entities such as the human soul, because they have no physical or material existence. Under these conditions, it seems hard to imagine how evil can actually exist. And if it does *not* exist, then how can God be blamed for permitting it?

In view of these factors, the very first step in this theodicy is to ask the atheist to justify the tools he is using to judge God for violating human rights or for being guilty of a moral crime, be it a crime of commission or of omission. The Christian worldview does not deny evil exists or that there is a universal standard of goodness against which something can be judged to determine if it is evil; these are central tenets of Christianity. What the Christian worldview asks is how an atheist can justify his use of those things without borrowing capital from the Christian worldview.

There is a sense, however, in which the Christian worldview invites the atheist or secularist to use capital from the Christian worldview in order to investigate Christian truth claims. The method of the Transcendental Argument for God's existence (TAG, as described in Chapter Six: *Yes, God Exists*) is to do an internal critique of non-Christian worldviews and look for the contradictions and inconsistencies which keep those worldviews from comporting with reality. While it is fair for a theodicy to point out the inconsistencies involved with atheists or secularists borrowing capital from the Christian worldview, it is equally appropriate to do an internal critique of the Christian worldview based on Christian presuppositions.

According to the Christian worldview, a contradiction is the hallmark of error. Christianity believes that there are rules of logic that are universal and invariable (not subject to change). Because laws of logic really exist and they are not human inventions (if they were human inventions everyone could make up their own logic), contradictions must not be ignored. A contradiction violates a law of logic regarding the relationship between two propositions. Consider these two propositions:

A) Barrack Obama was elected President of the United States in 2008.

B) Barrack Obama was not elected President of the United States in 2008.

There is a contradiction here, and that means one of these statements is in error, because they both cannot be true. If slavery, genocide or suffering reveals a genuine contradiction within Christianity, or if God has violated the human rights that He has mandated, then what the Christian worldview says about human rights is not credible. To thoroughly address each of these three issues could justify writing three separate books. For the purposes of this book, however, we will simply offer some basic answers intended to show that some skeptics have been hasty in their indictments against God.

The first issue to consider is slavery. In his book entitled *Letter to a Christian Nation*, avowed skeptic Sam Harris openly stated his goal of creating an internal critique of Christianity in order to destroy it. He states, "I have set out to demolish the intellectual and moral pretensions of Christianity."[99] After citing biblical texts which speak of the regulating of slavery, Dr. Harris states,

> "Nothing in Christian theology remedies the appalling deficiencies of the Bible on what is perhaps the greatest – and the easiest – moral question our society has ever had to face."
>
> (page 18)

It is common for critics to bring up the issue of slavery. Little attention is paid to the fact that slavery existed before Christianity or even before Judaism. The complaint is that the Bible failed to abolish slavery. This, we are told, makes God immoral, and as a consequence, God is more accurately called a violator of human rights than the source of human rights.

This theodicy has already pointed out the inconsistency of an atheist or secularist calling anything evil, since the atheist worldview cannot account for universal objective moral absolutes. Without those absolutes, morality is reduced to personal opinion and preference, nothing more. But the goal of this theodicy is

---

99   Sam Harris, *Letter to a Christian Nation* (New York: Alfred A. Knopf, 2006), p. ix.

not only to demonstrate the inconsistency of the atheist critique, it is also to point out the internal consistency within the Christian worldview based on its core presuppositions. The fact that a critic will not like the answer is irrelevant to the validity of the answer, validity that comes from internal consistency.[100]

The first thing that needs to be pointed out about slavery in the Bible is that it was completely different than modern conceptions of slavery. When Americans hear the word "slavery," they will naturally think in terms of the American experience with slavery. The conditions that characterized slavery in 1840 Mississippi were so different from Israel's experience in the Old Testament that anyone who would equate the two (something very common among modern skeptics/village atheists) forfeits all credibility. To read American slavery back into the Bible and then accuse God of supporting a moral evil based upon that flawed method is unfair and inaccurate.[101]

Jews were enslaved in Israel in order to pay off their debts. The majority of time this slavery was entered into voluntarily (Leviticus 25:39). These people were treated as members of the household and were to be set free at a regularly scheduled time (Deuteronomy 15:12). To kidnap someone and force him into slavery was a crime punishable

---

100   This is not to say critics are irrelevant. Every human soul is important; this is simply a reminder that a critic's personal dislike for the Christian answer does not count as a refutation.

101   American Christians living prior to the Civil War who tried to use the Bible to justify slavery had to break many rules of logic and sound Bible interpretation in order to do it. Modern critics of those Christians can point out their inconsistencies. However, the real test is not the imperfections of Christians, but the internal consistency within the Bible. God's Word will always pass such tests. Christians will attain perfection only in the next life. Until then, they are prone to make mistakes.

by death (Exodus 21:16). Israel had a strong sense of communal responsibility. Slavery was designed to protect the poor, to ensure that they had the basic necessities of life. This was probably the reason a daughter might be sold into slavery by her father – to deliver her from a situation of extreme duress. This treatment of slaves was vastly superior to the treatment of slaves in other nations.

Non-Jewish slaves who lived in Israel were also much better off than slaves in other nations. Israel had no facilities to house prisoners of war. Slavery preserved the lives of aliens, and they were granted legal protections. More than once, Israel was commanded by God to treat foreign slaves kindly and He reminded Israel that it had once been mistreated while enslaved in Egypt. Slaves that escaped from other nations were given refuge in Israel:

> *You shall not give up to his master a slave who has escaped from his master to you. He shall dwell with you, in your midst, in the place that he shall choose within one of your towns, wherever it suits him. You shall not wrong him.*
>
> Deuteronomy 23:15-16

By now, it should be obvious that the Old Testament commands regarding slavery were meant to extend mercy and protection.[102] New Testament standards reflect a similar ethic. To accuse God of condoning a moral evil is

---

102   This is a complex topic and we haven't looked at the New Testament. I recommend the website Christianthinktank.com and Glenn Miller's article, *Does God Condone Slavery in the Bible?* His extended treatment covers far more ground than is practical in this chapter.

unfounded. But let's take this further. Let's grant that slavery as practiced by Gentile nations throughout history has been a moral evil. So why didn't God put an end to it? Slavery, like every other moral evil, exists because of the sinfulness of the fallen human race.[103] Although God can choose to end evil at any time, He often chooses to use the sinful choices of man to bring about good.[104] In Genesis 37, Joseph's brothers sold him into slavery. This was an act of evil, but God brought good out of it. In Genesis 50:20, many years after his brothers' misdeed, Joseph testified to them, "You meant evil against me, but God meant it for good." The full story of Joseph is recorded in Genesis 37-50.

I believe the greatest good ever to come out of slavery is the redemption motif, which explains the sacrifice Jesus Christ made on the cross. The existence of slavery is more widespread than is commonly acknowledged. As a matter of fact, every human being alive today was or is, a slave to sin. Jesus proclaimed this in John 8:32-36, to people too proud to admit it:

"...and you will know the truth, and the truth will set you free." They answered Him, "We

---

103   Although the answer should be obvious at this point, the question can be asked, "On what absolute, objective basis can slavery be called evil? How is this possible in an atheist universe?" The Christian worldview can account for the moral absolutes which enable slavery to be criticized with something more than the individual, temporary, subjective, morally relative dislikes of the atheist. The Christian knows there is a universal and objective moral absolute that commands us to love our neighbor as oneself (Mark 12:31) and to treat others as we would want to be treated (Matthew 7:12). It is on this basis that we would judge slavery to be wrong.

104   According to Scripture, the day is coming when God will bring an end to all forms of evil on earth, and with it comes the judgment of God against all evil (Acts 17:31). It is a testimony of His patience and forbearance with sinful humanity that He has so far withheld the full measure of His judgment (II Peter 3:3-9).

are offspring of Abraham and have never been enslaved to anyone. How is it that you say, 'You will become free'?" Jesus answered them, "Truly, truly, I say to you, everyone who commits sin is a slave to sin. The slave does not remain in the house forever; the son remains forever. So if the Son sets you free, you will be free indeed".

When Jesus Christ suffered and died on the cross, He was paying the price of redemption:

In Him we have redemption through His blood, the forgiveness of our trespasses, according to the riches of His grace.

Ephesians 1:7

The concept of God's redeeming (purchasing, freeing) a people for Himself out of the hopeless bondage of slavery to sin is the main theme of the Bible. Indeed, to read the Bible without understanding the centrality of the slavery-redemption motif is to miss the point entirely. The pinnacle of the redemption motif is the glory of God (Ephesians 1:6-12; Revelation 5:9-12). This alone (the glory of God magnified by the redemption of sinners enslaved by sin) is sufficient reason for God's allowing sinful people the "freedom" to enslave one another.

It is very significant to note that the Greek word for "slave" or "bondservant" which is used in Ephesians 6:5 (*doulos*), is the same word which is applied to Jesus Christ in Philippians 2:7-8:

...but made Himself nothing, taking the form of a servant (doulos), being born in the likeness of men. And being found in human form, He humbled Himself by becoming obedient to the point of death, even death on a cross.

So thorough was Jesus' willingness to identify Himself with fallen humanity that He became a slave, even to the point of being bound and handed over to be executed (Mark 15:1). An especially poignant irony is that the 30 pieces of silver Judas Iscariot received for betraying Jesus was equivalent to the Old Testament value of a slave (see Exodus 21:32).

In light of the redemption motif, God's choice to permit slavery (He did not force men to enslave one another) is internally consistent with the biblical worldview and the moral perfection of God. It is my sincere hope that those who use the presence of slavery in the Bible to criticize God will have their eyes opened so that they will be set free from a slavery which is far worse than anything described in Ephesians 6:5.[105]

Why did God regulate slavery rather than eliminate it? We have already seen that the institution of slavery, which fallen men chose to impose upon one another, provided the motif for God revealing His plan to redeem

105   The skeptic who does not understand the frightful seriousness of his sin and his lost condition cannot appreciate the grace and mercy of the slavery – redemption motif. The classic hymn, *Amazing Grace*, contains these words: "Twas grace that taught my heart to fear, and grace my fears relieved." A critic might reject this theodicy because it does not fit with his presuppositions. But within the Christian worldview, there is internal consistency, and so we sing, "How precious did that grace appear, the hour I first believed."

sinners from slavery, and that every human being born into sin is already a slave (John 8:34). Spiritual slavery to sin is far worse than even the physical slavery men impose upon one another. The theology of God's redemption of man out of slavery to sin, and His moral improvements upon the conditions of physical slavery (see Galatians 3:28; Ephesians 6:9; Philemon 1:8-16), provided the moral impetus for the **Christian** Abolitionists of the nineteenth century who ended slavery in the Western world.

God's dealing with humanity takes into account that we live in a fallen world where moral perfection is not possible. An important parallel to slavery is polygamy. Like slavery, polygamy was contrary to God's beautiful creative purposes which reflected His holiness. From the beginning, God's plan for marriage was for one man and one woman to be joined together as husband and wife and for the two to become one (Genesis 2:21-25). Polygamy, like slavery, was a distortion of what God created and was brought about by sinful human choices. Polygamy first appeared in Genesis 4:19-24 and was clearly an act of defiance against God.

The practice of polygamy was common in the ancient world. God's people, even spiritual giants like Abraham and David, compromised with polygamy. Interestingly, every instance of polygamy among Israel's patriarchs recorded in the Old Testament brought heartache, division and regret. This was the consequence of going against God's creative purpose for marriage. However, in this fallen world where tragedies like slavery and polygamy exist, God chose to regulate these things. In Deuteronomy

21:15-17 God regulated polygamy even though it went against His ultimate purpose. This accommodation to fallen humanity is not a sign of His approval but of mercy! His patience should never be interpreted to be indifference toward sin or approval of it (II Peter 3:3-10).

Will skeptics accept this theodicy for slavery? Probably not, unless their hearts are close to being converted. They have a vested interest in putting God on trial and finding Him guilty. This is how people manage to suppress what they know about God's existence and His divine nature (Romans 1:18-20), and how they deal with a troubled conscience (Romans 1:32; 2:14-15). What this theodicy has done is to point out the internal consistency within the Christian worldview concerning God's willingness to permit (for now) the existence of things which are evil. The day is coming when God will judge and punish evil and immorality. I am thankful for His patience, because it afforded me the opportunity to repent and be forgiven prior to that day.

Finally, I cannot help but notice the irony of critics like the aforementioned Sam Harris in blaming the New Testament authors for not imposing anti-slavery morality upon the Roman Empire. Millions of people living in the Roman Empire did not find slavery either immoral or in need of reform. Should Christians have lobbied, protested and pressured Rome for legislation to reform slavery to the higher standards found in Galatians 3:28, Ephesians 6:9 and Philemon 1:8-16? Christians are opposed to abortion and find the killing of a baby within the mother's womb to be at least as immoral as slavery. But when Christians try to change prevailing laws to end abortion, they are told that it is wrong to impose their morality upon others. Apparently, such critics want to establish rules that will condemn Christians for imposing morality on American society (abortion) and for failing to impose morality on Roman society (slavery).

What about the problem of God's commanding genocide? Once again, the test is to determine if there is internal consistency within the Christian worldview. The Old Testament makes a strong distinction between murder and killing. Our tendency to blur distinctions because of sloppy thinking does not count against the Bible. The sixth commandment (Exodus 20:13) is a prohibition against "murder." This term refers to a premeditated intention to take an innocent life to satisfy the hate, greed, jealousy or malice of the murderer. Surrounding texts provide legitimate grounds for capital punishment (Exodus 21:12-14).[106]

The life being taken in these settings was not innocent, but was under the judgment of God. God ordained the human agency of government to carry out His judgment. This might involve killing, but it is not murder. If an armed criminal breaks into a house in order to harm its inhabitants and the homeowner defends her family with a gun and the intruder is killed, we consider that to be a legitimate act of self-defense, not murder. If a policeman kills the intruder, we consider that to be a

---

106 I will not try to justify capital punishment here. As already stated, the goal here is to simply show a logical consistency *within* the Christian worldview. I realize that those from outside the Christian worldview will have personal disagreements with many tenets of the Bible.

legitimate act of law enforcement, not murder.

In the case of the Midianites and the Amalekites, God determined to judge them for their wickedness.[107] As the Creator and Lord of the universe, God retains the right to judge individuals and nations, and to use human agents to carry out His judgment. In these instances, He used Israel.[108] Sometimes other nations were used by God to judge Israel when their idolatry and rebellion merited it (Jeremiah 5:15-17). If God's judgment of the Midianites and Amalekites seems harsh, we must once again ask for a justification of the objective moral absolutes against which God is judged and found wanting.

The real insight to be gained from these events is the hideousness and vileness of our sin in the eyes of a holy God. Few criminals ever believe their crimes are as serious as does the judge who sentences them. I have personally spoken with child molesters who felt they were the victims of unfair judges. This is a type of spiritual blindness that exists in the heart of every sinner. I am exceedingly grateful that a day came in my life when God, by His grace, filled my heart with sorrow for my sin and fear of His holiness. I am also grateful that in Him I found forgiveness. I have learned this is far preferable to minimizing my sin or of accusing God of being unjust in how He punishes sin.

God's judgment against the Midianites and

---

107   The extreme violence, immorality and idolatry of the ancient Canaanite nations is well documented. What they had done to so many others became the measure of judgment God used against them.

108   This does raise the question, "Who speaks (or judges) for God?" The fact that false prophets or mentally ill people can claim that God has authorized them to use force to judge others (something completely absent in the New Testament), does not negate the fact that God has the right to judge.

Amalekites also included His knowledge of the future. He not only knew of the sins which had been committed, He knew of the sins which would have been committed in the future by the present and succeeding generations. His knowledge is complete and exhaustive, and He knows every aspect of the actual and the potential. Think of a movie which is three hours in length. That represents 180 minutes or 10,800 seconds of film. Each second of the movie is comprised of many individual frames of film.[109] God knows all three hours in its entirety, from start to finish. At best, we have access to an individual frame of film here and there, and we see only still shots, while God sees the entire film in motion. His perspective is superior to mine and so I defer to His authority and His knowledge.

Our final concern is about the prevalence of suffering and evil in the world. Is the Christian worldview internally consistent given its presuppositions? The Bible teaches that when the world was originally created, God saw the work of His hands and called it "good" (Genesis 1:31). Death, disease, suffering and evil entered the picture only with the advent of sin (Genesis 3:16-19). All of the evil and suffering in this world is the consequence of sin. It is what the Bible refers to as the "curse." Even the very earth is under the curse, and that is why there are natural calamities that cause such suffering in the world.

The wonderful thing about the Christian worldview is the hope that it gives. Even when the curse for sin was originally pronounced, it was accompanied by God's promise that He would provide a Savior. The saving work

---

109   I recognize that changes in technology will soon make references to film outdated, but the illustration still works!

of Jesus Christ's death on the cross was foreshadowed in what the serpent was told, *"he shall bruise your head, and you shall bruise his heel"* (Genesis 3:15). When God clothed Adam and Eve with garments of animal skin in Genesis 3:21, it was a picture of an innocent substitute being provided as a covering/atonement for man's sin. That picture was fulfilled in Jesus, the Lamb of God who takes away sin (John 1:29). Someday, even the created world will be freed from the curse:

> *For the creation waits with eager longing for the revealing of the sons of God. For the creation was subjected to futility, not willingly, but because of him who subjected it, in hope that the creation itself will be set free from its bondage to corruption and obtain the freedom of the glory of the children of God.*
>
> Romans 8:19-21

It is also important to see that the Bible teaches that the evil God permits will ultimately accomplish a greater good for those who love Him. The greatest evil ever perpetrated was the execution of the Son of God, Jesus Christ, upon the cross. Men did evil and God permitted it:

> *Men of Israel, hear these words: Jesus of Nazareth, a man attested to you by God with mighty works and wonders and signs that God did through Him in your midst, as you yourselves know—this Jesus, delivered up according to the definite plan and*

foreknowledge of God, you crucified and
killed by the hands of lawless men.

Acts 2:22-23

There can be no greater evidence for God's plan to bring good out of the evil and suffering He permits than to consider the death of Jesus, a death that can save anyone willing to acknowledge Jesus Christ as Lord and Savior.

If we grant, for the sake of argument, that the theodicy presented here in this appendix is consistent with the teachings of the Bible, then it comes down to two basic options or choices. The two choices are portrayed in Elihu's speech found in Job 34:5-15. Option one is to critique God, as Job did, and find Him wanting.

Job says, "I am innocent, but God denies me
justice. Although I am right, I am considered
a liar; although I am guiltless, His arrow
inflicts an incurable wound".

Job 34:5-6

Option two is to agree with Elihu's assessment:

So listen to me, you men of understanding.
Far be it from God to do evil, from the
Almighty to do wrong. He repays a man
for what he has done, He brings upon him
what his conduct deserves. It is unthinkable
that God would do wrong, that the Almighty
would pervert justice. Who appointed Him
over the earth? Who put Him in charge of
the whole world? If it were His intention
and He withdrew His spirit and breath, all

mankind would perish together and man
would return to the dust.

Job 34:10-15

No theodicy has the inherent power to change the heart and mind of an unbeliever who prefers human autonomy over trust in God and obedience to Him. A properly constructed theodicy can, however, demonstrate that given Christian presuppositions, there are reasonable explanations for the evils and suffering that God permits. This is supplemented by the common human experience of encountering something which is painful, tragic or unfair, and at the point in time it happens, there seems to be nothing good which could come from it. With the advantage of hindsight (sometimes requiring years), however, we eventually are able to see the good which has come from that which was evil or painful.[110] Although there are many instances in which we will never see or perceive the good coming from an evil, it can be observed often enough to indicate that it is a very real phenomenon. Best of all, we have the testimony of Scripture:

But to all who did receive Him, who believed
in His name, He gave the right to become
children of God.

John 1:12

This is the Christian response to America's debate about rights.

---

110   Although God is obligated to keep His promises to the people to whom His promises are made (see Romans 8:28 and the promise that all things work out for the good), He is not obligated to those who are outside of the promise. This is yet another good reason to repent of sin and turn to Jesus Christ.

Chapter Eleven:

The Right To Eternal Life

I consider this chapter to be the most important one in this book. Do human rights matter? Yes, they do. Is the quality of life better when individuals and society respect God-given human rights and when government protects those rights? Yes, it is. But there is still something far more important than fundamental human rights. There is a special right, a right not possessed by all, because it is not something one is born with as he leaves his mother's womb. This right is not universal and it is not something a government can protect, nor is it something a government can violate. The right to which I refer is the right to become a child of God.

Let us consider once more the promise recorded in John 1:12-13:

But to all who did receive Him, who believed

in His name, He gave the right to become
children of God, who were born, not of blood
nor of the will of the flesh nor of the will of
man, but of God.

For our purposes, the key term in this passage is "right." The right that God bestows is the right to become His child.[111] This concept opens the door to a rich theology, for it is not sentimentality that is being expressed here. Before exploring this concept, I want to make the same distinction the Apostle John made in his Gospel. If you are a non-Christian reading this book, you are not God's child and you do not yet possess the right to become God's child. That is the bad news, and it is news that must be acknowledged before you can benefit from the good news.

There is something you need to understand. The bad news is not politically correct and it is not popular. The evangelical church in America has, as a general rule of thumb, done a poor job communicating the bad news to our culture. Too much attention has been paid to a marketing/advertising mindset that seeks to package the message of the gospel as though it is a product we want to sell to wary consumers. At times, it seems that some

---

111 Throughout this book we have defined a right as the "just power to make a moral claim upon someone." That definition works fine when dealing with other people (fellow creatures) or with governments. In John 1:12, the meaning is somewhat different, because no creature has the right to invoke a claim against the sovereign Creator. We do, however, have "the right" to expect God to be faithful to His own promises because He cannot lie (Numbers 23:19), and to expect Him to be true to His character because He cannot fail (Isaiah 51:6). Another facet of the right to become God's children is that death forfeits its hold over us, meaning we have the right to count death as a defeated enemy (I Corinthians 15:54-57). Some definitions of rights include the concept of a right as being the possession of a privilege. That definition works well with John 1:12.

Christian teachers and leaders have adopted a "give the customer what he wants" mentality. The problem with this approach is that human nature being what it is, no one wants to be told that he or she is a sinner, a criminal in God's universe and an object of His righteous wrath. Some churches shy away from delivering the bad news because not only is it unpopular, but people are also offended by it. If Jonathan Edwards (1703 - 1758) were alive today, he would not be invited to speak in very many churches unless he promised *not* to preach his most famous sermon, "Sinners in the Hands of an Angry God."[112]

Without excusing their silence, it is understandable why Christians can be reluctant to express the bad news found in the Bible. Imagine being a doctor who has learned that his patient has advanced cancer, the treatment of which is impossible for any methods known to modern medicine. No doctor would take delight in having to share such news. And then there is the patient: It is not unusual for someone who has received such news to go into denial. To do so isn't rational, but we can all understand the human capacity to believe that if we do not acknowledge the diagnosis, then it cannot hurt us. Of course, while we can understand the doctor's reluctance to tell the bad news and the patient's reluctance to accept the bad news, the news is not made better by either silence or denial.

So what is the bad news found in the Bible? We can answer that by considering our theme verse, John 1:12:

> ...*to those who believed in His name, He gave*
> ***the right*** *to become children of God...*

---

112   Jonathan Edwards was instrumental in the revival known as the Great Awakening, which deeply affected large portions of the American Colonies in the 1730s and 1740s.

There are monumentally important truths expressed and implied in these words. If being God's child is a right that must be given, then our natural state is not to have that right. In other words, left to ourselves, we are not God's children. That will come as an unwelcome shock to millions of people. Conventional wisdom and cultural conditioning have popularized the mistaken notion that we are all God's children.[113] Many people simply assume that the Bible must teach, somewhere within its pages, the universal brotherhood of man under the universal fatherhood of God. They likely also assume that anyone who would deny such a warm sentiment must be the kind of person who would relish stomping kittens, kicking puppies and stealing candy from young children.

Who would have the audacity to deny the proposition that we are all God's children? The answer to that question is Jesus Christ. John 8:12-59 reports a lengthy and pointed encounter that Jesus had with the Jews of Jerusalem. These Jews assumed they were God's children because they had descended from the patriarch Abraham. Because they were opposing His teaching, Jesus told the Jews that they were not truly Abraham's children. The Jews correctly understood Him to mean that they were therefore not God's children (8:34-41). The meaning of Jesus' words was very clear:

> *Jesus said to them, "If God were your Father,*
> *you would love me, for I came from God and*
> *I am here. I came not of my own accord, but*
> *he sent me. Why do you not understand what*

---

113   It can be said that God is the Father of all people, but only in His role as Creator (Psalm 24:1). There is no personal relationship with God on this level.

I say? It is because you cannot bear to hear my word. You are of your father the devil, and your will is to do your father's desires. He was a murderer from the beginning, and has nothing to do with the truth, because there is no truth in him. When he lies, he speaks out of his own character, for he is a liar and the father of lies. But because I tell the truth, you do not believe me. Which one of you convicts me of sin? If I tell the truth, why do you not believe me? Whoever is of God hears the words of God. The reason why you do not hear them is that you are not of God."

John 8:42-47

The more carefully we read Jesus' words in the New Testament Gospels the easier it is to understand why so many people wanted to kill Him. It was not just the Jews of John 8 who were outside of God's family, it is all of us. Unless we are given the right to become God's children, we will remain outside of His family, and when we die we will be eternally cut off from the heavenly home that awaits His children. We will be treated as our sins deserve, and that means Hell.[114]

All of this is bad news, but there is more. Some people are simply unwilling to admit that they are sinners.

---

114   It is not the purpose of this book to explain or defend the biblical doctrine of Hell. It is an important doctrine, but it goes beyond the scope of this book. For our current purposes, the following passages should be kept in mind: Matthew 25:41; Romans 2:5-9; Revelation 20:15. This is bad news, but it is not the whole story.

But among those people who are honest enough to admit their sins, there is a commonly held belief that enough good deeds can be done to compensate for any sins committed.[115] In other words, living a life in which the good outweighs the bad and obeying the Ten Commandments more often than not, should pretty much guarantee that things will turn out okay in the end. But John 1:12-13 makes no mention of human merit, effort or good works. The one thing Jesus refused to allow was the belief that any human could be good enough to merit forgiveness and to earn the right to become God's child. This human inability is included in the bad news, because it means that we are powerless to do anything to change our lost condition.

Did Jesus Christ teach that human deeds of goodness and kindness are of no saving value? Yes, that is what He taught. While many passages of Scripture could be cited, consider Luke 18:9-13.

> *He also told this parable to some who trusted in themselves that they were righteous, and treated others with contempt: "Two men went up into the temple to pray, one a Pharisee and the other a tax collector. The Pharisee, standing by himself, prayed thus: 'God, I thank you that I am not like other men, extortioners, unjust, adulterers, or even like this tax collector. I fast twice a week; I give tithes of all that I get'. But the tax collector, standing far off, would not even lift up his*

---

115   Usually the acknowledgement of sin is accompanied by a minimizing of its seriousness cf., "I'm not perfect, but at least I haven't killed anyone," or by favorably comparing ourselves to others cf., "I'm not perfect, but I would never do the things she has done." Jesus completely rejected these rationalizations.

eyes to heaven, but beat his breast, saying,
'God, be merciful to me, a sinner!' "

The first man in this parable was a Pharisee. Do not underestimate how serious the Pharisees as a people were about keeping God's law. This man was not lying about his actions. He really did refrain from stealing or committing adultery. He did fast and he did tithe. According to the things that can be measured outwardly by the human eye, the Pharisee had lived a better life than those around him. Although people today would not want to wear the label of Pharisee, many people would join the Pharisee in appealing to their goodness and listing the accomplishments that they believe deserve to be counted in their favor on Judgment Day.[116]

Now, what about the tax collector in Luke 18:9-13? He was more realistic about the bad news of sin, guilt and condemnation than was the Pharisee.[117] So aware was the tax collector of his lack of merit and goodness, that he would not even lift his head toward heaven. Instead, he beat his breast, a sign of remorse and sorrow. If you had asked the tax collector if he thought he was a child of God or if he had the right to be a child of God, he would have said no. As he considered both his own sinfulness and the

---

116   If you were to randomly ask 1,000 Americans, "Do you consider yourself to be a good person?" I have no doubt that a vast majority would say, "Yes, I am basically a good person." I have visited men in prison who had committed sexual crimes against children. These men, while admitting their guilt, still considered themselves to be "basically good."

117   If you are not familiar with the cultural significance of Jewish tax collectors in the New Testament era, you need to understand how they were viewed by others. Tax collectors participated in a system that bred corruption. Worst of all, they collected taxes for the hated Roman Empire. Respectable Jews refused even to associate with tax collectors (Matthew 9:10-11).

holiness of God, the tax collector recognized the news was bad.

Even if the tax collector had never committed another sin and spent the rest of his life doing good deeds, it was too late for him, just as it is for us. We are masters at minimizing the seriousness of our sin and our inability to merit God's forgiveness. Because God is perfect in His holiness and sinlessness, only that which is perfect can dwell in His presence. It is not enough that I might be "better" than a tax collector or that I have not committed the same wicked deeds as Adolph Hitler. Other people are not the standard against which we are measured. God is the standard, and He is perfect. That is why the bad news is true for everyone.

> *...for all have sinned and fall short of the glory of God...*
>
> Romans 3:23

Perfection is the standard. James 2:10 says that anyone who keeps the whole law yet stumbles at just one point is guilty of breaking the whole law. Such guilt can never be remedied by human effort. Now for the good news:

> *But to all who did receive Him, who believed in His name, He gave the right to become children of God, who were born, not of blood nor of the will of the flesh nor of the will of man, but of God.*

God freely offers what sinful man could never earn

or deserve. This offer, or gift, is what is referred to by the term "gospel" (good news). As the gospel is explained in the next several paragraphs, special attention will be paid to how key terms such as redemption, adoption, inheritance and citizenship lend themselves to rights talk.

Since America is the most rights-conscious culture in history, there is a great opportunity for Christians to use the concept of rights to build a bridge to the gospel. Instead of wringing our hands in despair over the misuse of rights in our culture, we ought to be excited about engaging our culture on the common ground of rights.[118] An example of this kind of dialog will be found in the following chapter (Chapter Twelve: "Two Friends Talk Some More").

Let us now consider the good news of Jesus Christ and how it can be understood in terms of rights. No claim is being made that the New Testament's teachings on redemption, adoption, inheritance and citizenship were primarily written to be a treatise on the rights that come with salvation. We must be careful not to read our own cultural norms back into the New Testament text. The original readers were not Americans who had grown up listening to the Beastie Boys sing "Fight for Your Right." Nevertheless, both Jews and Gentiles of the first century had a concept of rights (see Chapter Four: "And God Said, 'Let There Be Rights'").

---

118   There is a sense in which there is no common ground between the Christian worldview and the various worldviews of non-Christians. Because the Christian worldview presupposes the pre-eminence and Lordship of Jesus Christ as the foundation of all truth, this puts Christianity at odds with all alternative beliefs. However, because all people bear the image of God, there is a sense in which Christians share common ground with their non-Christian neighbors, and the nature of God-given rights invites meaningful dialog. The atheist has the same right not to be robbed and murdered as the Christian, but he can't truly account for that right.

It is fascinating to read the adventures of Paul as recorded in the Book of Acts and to see how Paul used his rights as a Roman citizen. Multitudes of people who lived in the Roman Empire were not citizens, but the advantages of citizenship were widely recognized. In Acts 16:12-40, we read the account of Paul's first visit to the city of Philippi, a Roman colony.[119] Paul's ministry in Philippi was fruitful, but it also met with violent opposition (Acts 16:16-24). Paul and Silas were beaten and imprisoned. The following day, the city magistrates, content that they had sufficiently punished these outsiders, ordered Paul and Silas to be released. It was then that Paul informed them of his Roman citizenship (Acts 16:37-38). The magistrates were badly frightened to learn that they had violated Roman law and had violated the rights that Paul had as a citizen. I do not believe Paul was thinking of his own interests, but that he was providing for the proper treatment of the Christian converts who would be the foundation of a new church once Paul left Philippi. The magistrates would think twice before they persecuted the new Christians, for they knew they were fortunate that Paul had not pressed charges against them. It is very significant that some time later, when Paul wrote to the Philippians, he talked about their citizenship being in Heaven (Philippians 3:20).

There were other occasions when Paul made use of his legal rights as a Roman citizen. Acts 21:15 – 23:11 is a detailed account of Paul's controversial visit to

119   Being classified as a Roman colony gave Philippi a privileged status. It was independent of regional authority and was modeled after Rome. Among its inhabitants were a significant number of legionnaires who had retired from the Roman Army.

Jerusalem. A riot broke out, and Paul would have been beaten to death by the angry Jews had not a detachment of Roman soldiers intervened. In the midst of this uproar, Paul again made use of his rights (Acts 21:39; 22:24-29). His arrest in Jerusalem led to Paul being transferred to Caesarea, where he was tried before the Roman governor of Judea, Felix (Acts 23:23 – 24:27). Paul eventually stood before Felix's replacement, Festus. It was on this occasion that Paul once again invoked his rights and appealed to Caesar (Acts 25:9-12). The book of Acts ends with Paul in Rome awaiting trial (Acts 28:14-31).

It should be noted that although Paul made use of his rights, the government officials that dealt with Paul were more concerned about upholding Roman law than about the rights of one man. This is a different emphasis than we see in contemporary American culture. For us, the rights of the individual are seen as being paramount, and the law, in some sense, serves the rights of the individual.[120] What is clear, however, is that the original authors and readers of the New Testament were capable of understanding the gospel in terms that included an awareness of rights.

One aspect of the gospel of Jesus Christ is that of redemption. The term "redemption," when used theologically, points to someone being purchased out of slavery. A slave does not possess the rights of someone who

---

120   I am speaking in very broad and general terms about a highly technical subject. It is not the purpose of this book to provide an in-depth explanation of the relationship between law and rights in the Roman Empire. Suffice it to say that, while there are parallels between the Roman and American systems, there are also significant differences.

is free. He or she is subject to the will of the slave-owner. Jesus taught that anyone who sins is a slave to sin (John 8:34-36), and lacks the privileges of sonship. Redemption from the bondage of sin is but one facet of the saving work of Jesus Christ on behalf of sinners. The redemption price paid by Jesus was His own life when He died on the cross for our sins (I Peter 1:18-19). When considering the promise of redemption, one cannot help but think of the speech of civil rights champion Martin Luther King who said from the steps of the Lincoln Memorial, "Free at last, free at last, thank God Almighty, I'm free at last."[121]

When someone comes to saving faith in Jesus Christ, he or she is legally adopted into God's family. The Romans had a richly developed system of adoption written into their laws. As Americans, we automatically think of adoption as involving young children and infants, but the Roman law provided for one adult to adopt another adult. This was primarily for the purpose of creating a legal heir for a man who had no heir. The 1959 Hollywood classic "Ben-Hur," which starred Charlton Heston and won eleven Academy Awards, includes a lengthy scene in which the hero, Ben-Hur, was made the legal heir of the Roman Consul, Quintus Arrius.[122] Although younger than the Consul, Ben-Hur was an adult. In teaching about the Christian's salvation, the Apostle Paul wrote to the Romans:

---

121   This is one of the most famous lines from Dr. King's memorable speech delivered on August 28, 1963. It is no coincidence that Dr. King connected theological concepts with civil rights.

122   The movie was based upon the1880 novel by Lew Wallace entitled, *Ben-Hur: A Tale of the Christ.*

For you did not receive the spirit of slavery
to fall back into fear, but you have received
the Spirit of adoption as sons, by whom we
cry, "Abba! Father!"

Romans 8:15

It is this adoption that makes Christians legal heirs of God (Romans 8:16-17).[123]

Redemption, adoption and inheritance are theological terms used to explain the gospel, and they imply the bestowing of rights, but there is more. Another biblical term is "citizenship." As already noted, Paul made use of the rights that were his as a Roman citizen. Granted, the rights of the individual citizen were a secondary consideration, it was the Roman law which was pre-eminent, but a citizen did have rights. Paul, writing to the Roman colony of Philippi, said:

But our citizenship is in heaven, and from it
we await a Savior, the Lord Jesus Christ...

Philippians 3:20

As you know, the title of this book is *The Rights Fight: A Christian Response to America's Debate About Rights.* One of the great political issues of our day is the issue of immigration. Should those who are in America illegally be granted amnesty and made citizens? Should they be given the rights of citizenship? The fact that such debates about citizenship are so visible and important in

<hr>

123   For further study on the relationship between the gospel and the vocabulary of rights, I highly recommend Francis Lyall, *Slaves, Citizens, Sons: Legal Metaphors in the Epistles* (Grand Rapids: Zondervan Publishing, 1984).

our political discourse should alert Christians to the rich opportunity to proclaim the gospel in our rights-conscious society.

Christians are a people redeemed from slavery and made free. They have been legally adopted by God and granted the rights of heirs. They have been given citizenship in heaven and all of the rights and privileges that come with that citizenship. All of this is by the grace of God. It is not deserved and it cannot be earned. The gospel rights of redemption, adoption, inheritance and citizenship are not inherent within us as a result of being born from our mother's womb. However, these rights are the result of a birth experience. Isn't this a contradiction? No, it is not. The birth that grants gospel rights is a second birth, rights that result from being born again. That second birth is described in John 3:3-8. Not everyone will experience this second birth; it is limited to those who have placed their faith in Jesus Christ, for He is the author of all true rights:

> *He was in the world, and the world was made through Him, yet the world did not know Him. He came to His own, and His own people did not receive Him. But to all who did receive Him, who believed in His name, He gave the right to become children of God, who were born, not of blood nor of the will of the flesh nor of the will of man, but of God.*

> John 1:10-13

This wonderful news should be at the center of a Christian response to America's debate about rights.

Chapter Twelve:

Two Friends Talk Some More

Once again, we will listen in on a conversation between Drew (Christian) and Neil (non-Christian). A few weeks have passed since their conversation in Chapter Seven: "Two Friends Talking." Shortly after this new conversation begins, Drew will recognize that there is an opportunity to share the gospel with Neil. An unfortunate circumstance has come into Neil's life regarding a question of rights. The main thesis of this book is that because the gospel can be explained in the context of rights, there will be many opportunities to share the gospel in a society as rights-conscious as America. Drew is concerned about Neil's immediate circumstances, which will come to light in this dialog, but he also cares about Neil's spiritual well-being. This conversation will address both of those concerns.

Drew:	So how was your vacation?
Neil:	That depends on how you look at it. We had a great time at the beach and the kids handled the drive well. The problem is in what I found when I got home.
Drew:	That doesn't sound good. What happened?
Neil:	Our house was broken into while we were gone.
Drew:	How did that happen?
Neil	Whoever it was broke in through the master bedroom.
Drew:	Did he go through the whole house?
Neil:	Fortunately, he only made it as far as the bedroom. You know my next door neighbor, Dennis. He checked on the outside of the house every night while we were gone. We figure that the break-in happened the night before we came home, and that Dennis must have come by while the crook was inside. Dennis never knew the crook was there, but the guy must have gotten spooked and taken off without going through the whole house.
Drew:	That thief was lucky he didn't run into Dennis, I don't think there would have been much left of him to turn over to the police.
Neil:	You're right about that!
Drew:	Neil, I'm sure having your house broken into is like a kick in the gut. I'm really sorry it happened. Did he manage to steal anything?
Neil:	Yah, part of my coin collection is gone.
Drew:	Oh, no! How did that happen? I know you keep

it locked up.

Neil: I do, and most of my collection is safe. But a couple of days before we left, I had my half-dollars out. Well, you know how it is. I had a ton of stuff I was trying to get finished before vacation and like an idiot, I never got around to locking those coins back up. I put them in a dresser drawer under some clothes. Apparently, the thief had just enough time to go through my dresser before Dennis came by.

Drew: Did he get the special coin?

Neil: My 1805? Don't remind me; it makes me sick to my stomach. Yah, he got it. My insurance agent says I'm covered, so I'll only be out a few hundred dollars, but I hate to lose that coin.

Drew: Maybe the police will be able to recover it for you.

Neil: I hope so, but it's a long shot. He probably traded it for drugs.

Drew: Is that what the police think?

Neil: Yes, they see it all the time.

Drew: Neil, I know you're bummed out about this, so we don't have to talk if you don't want to, but this incident relates to what we were talking about a few weeks ago.

Neil: You mean how could a loving God have let some thief steal my 1805 half-dollar for drugs?

Drew: That's not exactly what I had in mind.

Neil: I know. I just like giving you a hard time. Actually, I could use a good distraction, so go

	ahead and tell me what you're thinking.
Drew:	Okay, consider this. We instinctively think that the thief who broke into your home is some kind of lowlife. He not only stole from you but he also violated your living space and your family's home. In light of that, do you think an argument could be made that the thief had a right to take your coins?
Neil:	How could anyone possibly have the right to break into my house and steal my property? I could see it if I had stolen those coins from someone else and the rightful owner was trying to get them back. But those were *my* coins. I started collecting them with my grandfather when I was just a little kid.
Drew:	But isn't it at least possible that the thief was acting within his rights? I think I could make a pretty good case in his defense.
Neil:	This, I have to hear.
Drew:	Well, let's start with your house. Now I know you're not rich ...
Neil:	Not even close!
Drew:	No, but you are closer to being rich than some other people. You live in a nice house, you vacation at the beach and you have an expensive coin collection.
Neil:	All that's true. But it is also the case that I work about 50 hours a week and I'm careful with our money – we live within our means and we save as much as possible. And as far as my coin

collection is concerned, I've been working at it for twenty-five years and it is basically intended to put our kids through college. We figured we would have to sell the whole collection someday to do that, but I'm not complaining about it.

Drew: Well, if the thief who stole your coins is using the drugs he got for them right this very moment, then he feels fantastic. So, why shouldn't he be allowed to put his own desires above yours?

Neil: This is great! I have to listen to a Christian play Devil's advocate. I know you don't believe what you just said and this is some sort of lame attempt to argue for Christianity, but I'll play along. As far as the thief goes, I'm not denying him the right to live his own life as he sees fit, except when he crosses the line and violates my rights.

Drew: And what are your rights in this case?

Neil: At the very least I would say that I have the right to my own property, especially when it is inside my own home.

Drew: Why?

Neil: Why what?

Drew: Why do you have that right, if you have it at all?

Neil: Why do I have the right not to have my house broken into? Why do I have the right not to have my property stolen, property that would have been used to provide an education for my children? I know you well enough to know you're setting a trap for me, so I want a minute to think about this.

Drew: Sure, but it is a serious question with a lot of serious ramifications, I'm not trying to be funny.

Neil: Fine. I have a right to my property because I worked for it. I did not steal it from someone. Secondly, rights are necessary to provide stability and fairness to a society. We all agree that we don't want anarchy. I'm not asking for anything that I'm not willing to give someone else. I will respect my neighbor's property, so this is nothing more than equal treatment. We are all better off when people respect each other's rights. It is as simple as that.

Drew: I knew it! You are a man of great faith. You have far more faith than I do.

Neil: Meaning what?

Drew: Neil, your answer is filled with assumptions that you haven't proven and which need to be tested. You say that you have a right to your property because you worked for it rather then stole it. But why should that matter? What would you say to the thief if he said, "I have a right to these coins because I stole them without getting caught?"

Neil: Not getting caught doesn't make those coins his property. There's no legal basis for that.

Drew: What if we changed the law? What if a provision was made that said as long as you don't get caught, any property you steal becomes yours?

Here's something to think about: The day after he stole your coins, the thief had a friend over to his apartment. His friend noticed the 1805 half-dollar on the kitchen table and tried to sneak it into his pocket. But your thief saw what his friend was trying to do, stopped him and said, "Take your hands off that, it's mine!" In that instance, I'll bet your thief really believed that it's his coin. So, does mere possession of an item bestow a right?

Neil: Not in this case. I'm still the rightful owner.

Drew: Okay, then let's get back to the law. Last month, the law was changed so it now includes a provision that as long as you don't get caught, any property you steal becomes yours. Your thief was not caught, so the 1805 half-dollar is now legally his. Do you agree that the coin is no longer rightfully yours?

Neil: Nope. It's still my coin.

Drew: But on what basis can you say that? It is no longer in your possession and, according to the law, it now belongs to the thief.

Neil: Nobody's going to pass a stupid law like that.

Drew: But what if they did? Wouldn't you then lose your right to the 1805 half-dollar, and wouldn't the thief now be the rightful owner? When you call such a law stupid, I think what you're saying is that the law is unjust. Would you call this new law unjust?

Neil: If it gives my 1805 half-dollar to some thief

	who broke into my house and stole a coin I was saving for my children's education then, yes, I would call it unjust.
Drew:	So it's unjust. We would both agree that many unjust laws have existed in the past. Who is the rightful owner of the coin?
Neil:	I am.
Drew:	But look at this from the thief's point of view. The coin is in his possession and the law says he is the rightful owner. It is his by legal right. Who are you to deny him his legal right?
Neil:	I know you think you're clever, but it's time for a reality check. A society that made the kind of law you are suggesting would eventually destroy itself. Such a system can't work and it isn't practical. People eventually figure stuff like that out and make the necessary adjustments.
Drew:	So maybe the law that makes the thief the rightful owner of the 1805 half-dollar will turn out to be impractical and it will be changed thirty or forty years from now. But as of now, this very moment, who is the rightful owner?
Neil:	I still think it's mine.
Drew:	Well, if it is, then you've just admitted that the right to property can't always be established by possession or law or practicality. Furthermore, we can look at recent history and see that unjust laws are common. Neil, let me shift gears and ask you three questions: What is a right, where

do rights come from and how do you know?

Neil: I'll tell you what. I'm going to pull a reverse on you. I'm going to ask *you* those questions and poke holes in your answers. So, Drew, let me ask you: What is a right, where do rights come from and how do you know?

Drew: There's more than one way to define a right, and it depends on whether you are talking about a universal human right or a legal right that has been created by statute. But on the most basic level, I would say that a right is the just power to make a moral claim upon someone. I believe you have the right to keep your personal property. You have the just power to tell the thief that he has no right to your coins and you have the right to enlist the help of the police to protect your property. But, Neil, here's the most important thing to recognize about that definition. When I use the word "just," I am claiming there is a standard of justness or justice that both you and the thief are subject to. It isn't about who has more power, or who can write the laws that serve his own ends. Your right is just, so the power you use to protect or enforce that right is something other than raw power or overwhelming power. There is a moral quality to that power, which is why I say it is a "just" power.

Neil: I'm tracking you so far, but I still have questions.

Drew: We'll get there, Neil, I promise. But let me finish

this first answer. The thief who stole your coins does not have the just power to make a moral claim on you, even if the law were to say that it is okay for him to steal. That would be an unjust law. In other words, a good law might acknowledge or protect your right to property and a bad law might deny or deprive you of the free exercise of your right to property, but human law itself is not the ultimate authority and is not the ultimate source of your right to property. The real authority comes from that which is "just." Both you and the thief are measured by what is just. But that position seems to create an even bigger problem, doesn't it?

Neil: What do you mean?

Drew: Who gets to say what the standard for "justness" is? At this point, we are talking about something more than legality; we are talking about morality. A few minutes ago, I explained that the thief thinks the 1805 half-dollar is his because he successfully stole it from you and because of the new law that says anyone who steals without getting caught becomes the legal owner. When I asked you who the rightful owner is, you still thought it was your coin. You are looking beyond legality and appealing to morality. Your claim is that the thief is in the wrong and the law that protects him is unjust. But unless there is a universal, unchanging and objective standard for morality, all you are really doing is stating your personal preference. You still prefer to be regarded as the owner of that coin and by your personal moral standards, you feel justified in that preference. And the thief will answer that according to his personal moral standards, he is the owner of the coin; plus, he can exercise the legal power to enforce his ownership against you. I'm sorry, Neil, but that's where moral relativism leaves us. Are you still sure you want to live in an atheist universe?

Neil: Before I respond to that, I want to hear your answer to the other two questions, "Where do rights come from and how do you know?"

Drew: Those two answers are directly related to my first answer. Since a right is the just power to make a moral claim upon someone, those rights have to come from God. We have seen that the key word is "just," which alerts us to the fact that we are looking beyond mere legality and into the realm of morality. Certainly, there are legal issues connected to rights, but the word "just" is a measurement or standard of morality. Let's use your coin as an example. Is there a basic human right to own property and to not have that property stolen by a common thief? If you base morality on a secular or humanistic foundation, then we have to admit that the right to own property is someone's subjective standard. It might even be the standard of the majority. But it is still man-made, local and subject to change. If 51 percent of a community decided to deprive 49 percent of a community of their property, and justified it on the basis of the needs of the majority, would this be morally wrong? No. It would be one particular community's moral code, and it is relative to their circumstances and values. Who are you to judge them by your own equally subjective and relative moral standards? There is no universal, absolute and objective human right to private property. The only right to property is that which is created by law. In an atheist universe, all rights have to be created by man-made law, because there can be no universal, objective rights or moral standards. And if the source of your rights is human law, then you don't have a leg to stand on when a new law takes those rights away. And that includes the case of your 1805 half-dollar.

Neil: Do you need to catch your breath?

Drew: Don't stop me; I'm on a roll.

Neil: Okay, I understand what you're saying. A right is the just power to make a moral claim on someone, and for that definition to make sense I need to look to God. That much is reasonable, so I'm not going to be obstinate about it. However, I see two huge problems with what you're saying. Why do I have to accept your definition of a right, and how do you know God exists?

Drew: You don't have to accept my definition, but I think that by your own words, you have given evidence you know in your heart it is true. When I described the thief who stole your coin as now being the rightful owner of the coin, you protested. You insisted that no matter what the law said, you are still the owner. Neil, I'm asking you to be consistent. Either give up your claim to that coin or acknowledge that the most essential human rights involve having a just power to make a moral claim, and that requires what only God can give. You will never find it in an atheist universe. Yes or no, are you still the rightful owner of that coin?

Neil: Just because there's a logical consistency in what you're saying, doesn't mean it is true.

Drew: Well, considering that a few weeks ago you accused Christianity of requiring a blind leap of faith, I think we are making progress.

Neil: Don't get your hopes up.

Drew: My hopes are always up for you, Neil, because my wife and I pray for you and for your family every day.

Neil: Even though I doubt there is anyone on the receiving end of those prayers, I know you mean well and I appreciate it. And that reminds me; you answered the first two questions, but not the third. You say that a right is the just power to make a moral claim on someone. You also claim that rights come from God, at least universal human rights. But the third question is, "How do you know?" I can see that you have made a strong case for the logical necessity of God's existence, if there are universal human rights. But so what? I'll just assume that universal human rights don't exist. I'm sure there are legal experts or philosophers who will argue that the universal human rights Christians believe in are an illusion, but that we can create a workable system of rights ourselves without having to make an appeal to God. Therefore, there is no logical necessity for God's existence. You lose.

Drew: Neil, it is sad to see how much you are willing to give up just so you don't have to acknowledge God. But, as a friend, I want to respectfully point out that while you profess to live in an atheist universe, you can't really live that way. Something inside of you knows that you are the rightful owner of the half-dollar, and no man-made system can alter that reality. On point after point, you keep borrowing capital from the Christian worldview even while outwardly professing not to believe in God. It is God who grants you the right to own property. When that thief stole your coins, he was violating one of the Ten Commandments; "You shall not steal." You have a court of appeal and it is God's court. Even if every human court sides with the thief, you can still call it an injustice without being inconsistent, because human courts are not the ultimate authority or standard. The God-given right to own property *is* important, but there is a far more important right that can be yours. Can I talk to you about it?

Neil: I suppose you're going to say something about the right to life.

Drew: I am, but probably in a way much different than you anticipate.

Neil: Okay, just don't take all day.

Drew: Neil, you are correct that I believe there is a universal human right to life, and it is protected by God's commandment, "You shall not murder." You possessed that right the moment you were conceived, because you bear the image of God. I have a duty not to murder you, because you have a right not to be murdered. You were born with that right and it will always be yours. That doesn't mean people will always respect it, because there are murderers out there just like there are thieves who steal coins, but it is your right. However, Neil, I possess a right to life that you don't have.

Neil: What was that? Did I just hear what I think I heard?

Drew: Yes, you did. I have a right to life that I was born with. It can never be taken away, and unlike your right to life, mine can never be violated by someone else. It is absolutely secure.

Neil: Are we talking about the same thing?

Drew: Excellent! You picked up something I said. If it sounds to you like I am talking about two different types of the right to life, you're correct. The first right to life is the one you and I were both born with. You have the right not to be murdered by me, and I have the right not to be murdered by you. We are both thirty-five years old, so we have had this right for the same amount of time and will continue to have it for the rest of our lives. If we live to be eighty, we will possess the right to life for another forty-five years. But, Neil, I have another right to life which you lack, and I was born with it. Can I tell you about it?

Neil: I insist.

Drew: This second right to life has only been mine for the last ten years.

Neil: Wait a minute. You just said you were born with it.

Drew: I was born with it ten years ago. Now, since that doesn't seem to make sense, I need to explain what I mean. Neil, one of my favorite passages in the Bible is found in John 1:10-12. It talks about believing in Jesus Christ and this is what it says:

> *He was in the world, and the world was made through Him, yet the world did not know Him. He came to His own, and His own people did not receive*

Him. But to all who did receive Him,
who believed in His name, He gave the
right to become children of God.

The right to become a child of God results from having experienced a second birth. In John 3:3, Jesus said it like this:

Jesus answered him, "Truly, truly, I
say to you, unless one is born again he
cannot see the kingdom of God."

Neil: Are you talking about Heaven?

Drew: In a sense, yes. Jesus once said that He is the resurrection and the life and that whoever believes in Him will live eternally, even though he might die in this present life. You can read those words in John 11:25-26. Eternal life is what we receive when we are given the right to become children of God.

Neil: So some people have that right, and some don't?

Drew: Yes. The right itself is not universal, not everyone has it.

Neil: Are you saying you're better than I am?

Drew: Actually, Neil, I would say almost the exact opposite. Another man who wrote parts of the Bible was named Paul. In the letter that we call I Timothy, Paul wrote this:

The saying is trustworthy and
deserving of full acceptance, that
Christ Jesus came into the world
to save sinners, of whom I am the
foremost. But I received mercy for this

reason, that in me, as the foremost, Jesus Christ might display His perfect patience as an example to those who were to believe in Him for eternal life.

I see my sinfulness the same way Paul saw his. So, no, I don't consider myself better than you. I have not been given the right to become a child of God because I am better than you or anyone else. I could never deserve it or earn it. And the good news is that God doesn't ask us to earn this right. It is given as a gift to all who believe, and that's actually why some people won't accept it.

Neil: What do you mean?

Drew: One of the reasons God doesn't ask us to work our way to Heaven is because we are incapable of doing it. God is perfectly holy and without sin. He can't change or deny His own character, so that means He can't accept anyone into Heaven who is less than perfectly holy and is not without sin.

Neil: But you just admitted to being a sinner, yet you think you're going to Heaven. Isn't that a contradiction?

Drew: Great question, Neil! No, it isn't a contradiction, because God has provided for me the goodness or sinlessness which I lack and could never attain by my own efforts. That provision is a part of God's gift to me through Jesus Christ. Jesus came to earth and lived a perfect and sinless life.

The Bible tells us that Jesus died on the cross to pay for my sins, not His, for He had no sin. Jesus was sentenced to die on the cross, a punishment reserved for the worst of criminals. It wasn't a just sentence, but Jesus set aside His right to justice because of His love for me. When He died as a criminal, it was as though He took my place. That's how God considers Jesus' death – as full payment for my sin so I can be acquitted. But the one thing God requires of someone before that person will be given the right to become a child of God is the one thing that keeps people away.

Neil: What's that?

Drew: You have to admit that you need to be given this right as a gift, because you can't ever be good enough to earn it. Most people consider themselves to be basically good and they think that if there is a scale that weighs the good versus the bad, their good outweighs their bad and that makes them good enough to go to Heaven. It boils down to pride in one's own goodness. Most people are unwilling to admit that they fall short and that their good works contribute nothing to changing their guilt before God. God calls us to come to Him through faith alone, in Christ alone, and all this is by God's grace alone. Neil, would you like to trust in Christ to save you right now?

Neil: How did we go from talking about my stolen coins to you preaching a sermon about Heaven? You've given me much to think about, and that's exactly what I want to do – think about it.

Drew: Neil, I hope you will end up believing and trusting in Christ. I hope I can persuade you of that, but I would never want to pressure you into that decision. What you decide is between you and God. Please know that I am always available to talk some more.

~ ~ ~ ~ ~

We will leave Drew and Neil at this point. There were two central issues in this dialog, each of which could encompass hundreds of pages and still not be fully discussed. The first issue was Neil's right to property, namely the coins which were stolen from him. The second issue was Drew's presentation of the gospel, which grew out of the discussion about rights. The case of Neil's coins having been stolen and Drew's ability to turn the theft into an opportunity to present the gospel might seem unrealistic, contrived and unlikely in a real-world conversation. To some degree, that might be true, but we do live in a society in which people take their rights very seriously and the gospel can be presented in terms of rights. Such opportunities can be found, if Christians will learn to look for them and create them.

In the introduction to this book, I stated that my goal was to offer an apologetic, which I consider a reasoned defense, for the biblical view of the divine origin of rights. I have offered this apologetic for five reasons:

1) A passion for God's glory and the desire to see

His authority be proclaimed and understood.

2) A burden to see Christians be equipped to share the gospel effectively in a rights-intoxicated culture.

3) A desire to see Christians strengthened in their faith.

4) A love for my children and the desire to see them live in a society safeguarded from secular and religious tyranny.

5) A love for my neighbors and a desire to see them live in a society safeguarded from secular and religious tyranny.

The third goal, seeing Christians have their own faith strengthened, is important even if it never leads to an evangelistic encounter patterned after the model proposed in this book. Apologetics can be a very useful tool in evangelism, but often the greatest benefit that comes from the study of apologetics is in what it does for the Christian. Throughout the 2,000-year history of Christianity, the need for believers to be strong and courageous has been constant. If there was ever a period of time in American history when openly practicing and proclaiming the Christian faith was relatively easy, that time has come to an end. Christians who are unwilling to embrace and endorse legal rights that directly conflict with the Christian faith will, with ever greater frequency, find themselves standing in the same place as the apostles when they were threatened by the Sanhedrin in Acts 5:27-42.

May God grant that Christians will take hold of the

opportunities for apologetics and evangelism that come with living in a culture which has a constantly growing appetite for an ever-increasing number of rights claims. And as they seize those opportunities, may Christians share, with great joy and with a love for their neighbors, this message:

He was in the world,
and the world was made through Him,
yet the world did not know Him.
He came to His own,
and His own people did not receive Him.
But to all who did receive Him,
who believed in His name,
HE GAVE THE RIGHT
to become children of God.

Appendix A:

The Lucas – Allen Debate

On a February weekend in 2005, the church on whose staff I serve, Grace Community Church of Washington Court House, Ohio, hosted *The Worldview Conference*. It was an enjoyable time, and I was gratified that our speakers included Dr. Edwin Yamauchi (Miami University of Ohio), Dr. Bill Brown (President of Cedarville University), Dr. John White (Athletes in Action) and our worship leader, Steve Camp. They all did a wonderful job in presenting facets of the Christian worldview. The conference began with a formal debate on the existence of God, and I had the privilege and the responsibility of speaking for Christian Theism. The transcript of my opening presentation follows shortly.

Several months before the conference, I had contacted an atheist activist to inquire about his interest in participating. He was Mr. Michael Allen, who was serving as the Ohio State Director of American Atheists. Michael was enthusiastic, and we had no difficulty settling on debate protocol. His willingness to debate added an exciting dimension to the conference, and I greatly appreciated his congenial attitude.

My opening presentation in the debate with Michael was based on my understanding of Scripture and Dr. Greg Bahnsen's Transcendental Argument for God (TAG). Let me be quick to acknowledge that even on my best day, I could never hope to rise to the level of Dr. Bahnsen, even if I simultaneously caught him on his worst day. My presentation was similar to the way in which Dr. Bahnsen taught TAG, but not identical to it, and any flaws in my presentation should not be attributed to him.

One final but important consideration: Of the 800 people who were in attendance for the debate, a significant portion, perhaps even a majority, were members of Grace Community Church. Before, during and after the debate, they were gracious, warm and very hospitable. Considering the nature of the event, the friendly atmosphere they created was a true testimony of Christian love and humility. The apologetic value of their testimony was perhaps even more important than anything I had to say.

Here was my opening presentation:

Good evening. I want to thank each of you for being here tonight, and I certainly want to thank Michael for his kindness in our many communications.

Why am I here tonight? Like many of you, I have

a thirst for knowledge and, having met with Michael, I know that he will be very helpful as I seek to sharpen my thinking. But I can think of at least two motives more important than mere intellectual curiosity. First of all, I love God and I want His name to be declared and glorified, for this is the highest purpose one can have in life. Secondly, I care about each of you as individuals and I definitely care about Michael. This is a practical application of my Christian worldview. The God who created us can be personally known, and to know Him is to know the source of all life and truth.

In keeping with the stated purpose of this debate tonight, I would like to give you a reason for the hope that is within me. The question which has been posed is, "Does God exist?" In other words, is there a God and how can we know? I would like to begin my answer, which will be in the affirmative, by stating three basic factors. First, we need to start with a definition. The God of Christian Theism is, by way of a simple working definition, the eternally self-existent Creator of the universe, and He is both transcendent to it and immanent within it. God has made himself known to us through the general revelation of the created order, the special revelation of the Scriptures and, most importantly, through the incarnation of the Son of God, Jesus Christ.

Second, I want you to know up front that my opening argument will not give a lot of consideration to the evidences presented by Christian apologists such as Josh McDowell and Gary Habermas, evidences which support the historical reliability of the Bible and the miraculous resurrection of Jesus Christ. What about evidences for the creation account of Genesis offered by scientists like Duane Gish, or intelligent design advocates such as William Dembski? An abundance of such evidence is available, but I do not start with it because such an approach ignores the more fundamental clash of worldviews and the presuppositions upon which worldviews are built. A person's worldview will determine how he or she interprets evidence for or against the existence of God, so listing evidences is not the place to begin.

I believe it is more constructive to argue for the existence of God by critiquing worldviews as a whole, rather than taking individual snippets of evidence, the interpretation of which is actually controlled by the worldview of the person looking at the evidence. This awareness of worldviews is the third controlling factor in my presentation tonight. I have a worldview and so does Michael and so do all of you. A worldview is the core set of beliefs and assumptions a person has by which he interprets all that he experiences in life.

By focusing on worldviews, I hope that we can avoid the chimpanzee syndrome. What I mean by this is the process by which an atheistic evolutionist observes the similarity between the DNA of a chimpanzee and that of a man and says, "Aha, evidence of a common ancestor." A special creationist looks at the exact same evidence and says, "Aha, evidence of a common Creator." The two conclusions are completely opposite, yet they are perfectly consistent within the worldview of each man and each man is frustrated by what he perceives to be the close-mindedness of the other.

On the Ohio Atheists' Website, Michael has stated that he rejects Christian Theism because he claims it offers him no evidence. The problem is that his worldview excludes any evidence that doesn't fit with his atheism. Ironically, his worldview can't even account for the dynamic of evidential reasoning.

Well, then, what should we do? If all the evidence I offer Michael will be unpersuasive because he filters it through an atheistic worldview, and if I reject Michael's arguments because of my theistic worldview, is there any hope of a truly meaningful debate tonight? In a sense, we each wear worldview sunglasses. All that I see is tinted by the glasses I wear and my brand of sunglasses is Christian Theism. All that Michael sees is colored by his worldview sunglasses, which are decidedly not Christian Theistic. Someone might suggest that we should each take off our worldview glasses and in the spirit of neutrality, examine the evidence objectively. In other words, let's simply follow the dictates of reason and if theism isn't reasonable, let's reject it or if atheism isn't reasonable, we'll reject that.

I don't believe that such neutrality is possible, and feel that it is naïve to proceed as though it is. I do agree, however, that reason ought to be brought to bear on the question of God's existence. Guess what? If you agree with the approach that says reason is possible and essential, it shows that rather than being neutral or atheistic, you are thinking in accordance with the Christian worldview. As a matter of fact, my central argument tonight is that for Michael to use reason and the laws of logic, he must borrow from my worldview. The Christian worldview provides a basis for reason and logic, whereas, if atheism were true there could be no such thing as reason or the laws of logic, laws of science, objective moral values and even human rights. In a very real sense, Michael lost tonight's debate the moment he decided to be a part of it.

What I am submitting for your consideration is what is known as the Transcendental Argument for the existence of God. Basically, the Transcendental Argument for God is that He is the necessary precondition if there is to be any intelligibility of reason, the laws of logic, the laws of science and objective moral values. Both my worldview and Michael's worldview make use of reason, logic, science and ethics. On that, I think we can agree. My contention is that my worldview can account for these things, while Michael's cannot. Thus, atheism is internally incoherent and cannot account for human experiences, whereas Christian theism is consistent. Thus, when it comes to critiquing the evidence you hear tonight, my worldview sunglasses can be trusted and Michael's cannot.

Consider the basic premise of atheism. If the universe is atheistic, it is nothing more than matter in motion. It is natural, not supernatural. It is wholly material in nature, with no immaterial entities. In other words, a naturally occurring material or physical universe does not allow for the existence of a supernatural, immaterial or non-physical God. Not only is there no currently existing microscope under which we can put a sample of God, no such microscope could ever be devised, for the very essence of God is outside of nature and matter. Scientists are fond of telling us that no supernatural explanations are permitted. To posit God as an explanation of phenomena which occurs in a natural, material universe is to make a non-statement which cannot explain anything.

The problem with the atheist's universe is that it eliminates more than God; it also eliminates reason, the laws of logic, the laws of science, objective moral values and any hope of an understanding of the human mind which is not absurd. This is because a universe which is strictly material in nature cannot account for any of these things. "But wait just a minute," someone might say. "Atheists are committed to the use of reason, logic, science and ethics. Many of the greatest scientific advances have come from atheists and many atheists lead morally admirable lives, surpassing that of many professing Christians I know."

Now, I certainly don't deny that atheists do all these things, but by their use of reason, logic, science and ethics, they are actually showing that in their hearts they know the God who created them, for these things make sense in the Christian worldview but not in the atheist world. You see, in the Christian worldview there can be things such as universal abstract laws and the laws of logic, which means that one truly can reason. In the Christian worldview there are immaterial realities and objective moral absolutes. There is a God who orders the universe so that we can expect a uniformity of experience which provides the basis for making predictions, the linchpin of empirical science.

One way of summarizing the proof for the existence of God is by showing the impossibility of the contrary.

If there is no God, we have no basis for believing there are such things as the laws of logic, the uniformity of nature, objective moral values or human minds which can genuinely discover truth. And if there is no basis for these things, why are we even having this debate? It is because both Michael and I believe in logic, reason, science and ethics. But as I have stated, a universe which is only matter in motion cannot produce such realities. So we are left with the ironic situation of atheists borrowing from the Christian worldview and then turning around and denying the validity of that worldview.

If you are not familiar with the Transcendental Argument for the existence of God, some of my assertions tonight might strike you as odd, so perhaps in a later segment we can explore it in more depth. For now, I will take my last few minutes to consider the inadequacies of atheism in the realm of objective moral values.

On November 2, 2003, Michael posted on the Ohio Atheists Website a transcript of his opening remarks from a debate in which he had participated earlier that day. In that debate, Michael expressed disapproval over what he believes to be the dishonesty of scientific creationists. Clearly, Michael believes that those involved in debate have an obligation to be honest and truthful. I share that sense of obligation. I also think that most, if not all, of you came here tonight with the expectation that both Michael and I would be honest in our arguments. I'm sure Michael expects me to be honest and would see it as obligatory in a debate such as this. We both agreed several months ago on the parameters of tonight's debate, and Michael is justified in viewing me as being under obligation to keep my word, justified, that is, if he borrows from my worldview, that is. For in the Christian worldview when a person gives his word, he is obligated to keep it and to be a liar is not simply impolite, it is genuinely wrong. In an atheist world, there can be no such thing as universal objective moral absolutes by which I can be judged to be in the wrong, no matter how egregious my lies.

In that same debate Michael declared, "I feel like truth is the most fundamental value one can have, and without it, it is difficult to go further. In order to talk about anything, including values, including Jesus or holy ghosts or speaking in tongues, I have to establish first that that I'm being honest about what I am saying, and I have to establish that I value, not just lip service to truth, but the actual rational processes by which we separate truth from fiction."

My question for Michael is, does he value truth merely because he finds it useful, or because it is morally right? If it is merely useful, he has no complaint against those who find dishonesty useful for their purposes. If I engage in a series of lies here tonight, I believe Michael has just two logical responses available to him. He can . . .

a) Justly condemn my behavior by holding me to an objective universal standard. Of course, to do this he will need to use my worldview, the very thing he denies.

Or, he must ...

b) Protect atheism by denying the existence of objective universal standards.

But not only will this render him unable to condemn my lying, the absence of objective universal moral laws reduces Michael to silence in response to the atrocities of Hitler and Stalin, as well. If someone objects by saying my argument is simply inflammatory, I would have to take such a response as a failure to deal with the logic of my challenge.

Aldous Huxley rejected Christian Theism and its moral absolutes. When he worked this out in his personal philosophy he had this to say:

> I had motive for not wanting the world to have a meaning; consequently assumed that it had none, and was able without any difficulty to find satisfying reasons for this assumption. The philosopher who finds no meaning in the world is not concerned exclusively with a problem in pure metaphysics, he is also concerned to prove that there is no valid reason why he personally should not do as he wants to do, or why his friends should not seize political power and govern in the way that they find most advantageous to themselves ... For myself, the philosophy of meaninglessness was essentially an instrument of liberation, sexual and political.

If you don't like what Huxley is saying and wish to reject it, you must first reject atheism, for although many atheists may personally dislike Huxley's morality, atheism provides no objective means for condemning it. This dilemma is painfully obvious in the *Second Humanist Manifesto* of 1973. The Manifesto openly espouses atheism yet would also reject Huxley's version of ethics. The Manifesto says:

> We affirm that moral values derive their source from human experience. Ethics is autonomous and situational, needing no theological or ideological sanction. Ethics stems from human needs and interests. To deny this distorts the whole basis of life.

Further on in the Manifesto is a treatment of human sexuality which includes these propositions:

> In the area of sexuality, we believe that intolerant attitudes, often cultivated by orthodox religions and puritanical cultures, unduly repress sexual conduct ... While we do not approve of exploitive, denigrating forms of sexual expression, neither do we wish to prohibit, by law or social sanction, sexual behavior between consenting adults. The many varieties of sexual exploration should not in themselves be considered "evil." Without countenancing mindless permissiveness or unbridled promiscuity, a civilized society should be a tolerant one. Short of harming others or compelling them to do likewise, individuals should be permitted to express their sexual proclivities

and pursue their life-styles as they desire. We wish to cultivate the development of a responsible attitude toward sexuality, in which humans are not exploited as sexual objects, and in which intimacy, sensitivity, respect, and honesty in interpersonal relations are encouraged.

Did you catch the glaring contradiction? The Manifesto denies all grounds for moral absolutes by embracing situation ethics, yet turns around and establishes its own moral absolutes. It rejects the restrictions orthodox religion places on sexual conduct as being "unduly repressive." Then it turns around and places its own limits on sexual behavior promoting:

"the development of a responsible attitude toward sexuality in which humans are not exploited as sexual objects, and in which intimacy, sensitivity, respect and honesty in interpersonal relations are encouraged."

But why in an atheist universe do I have to accept those limits? What if I find it personally satisfying to be exploitive? What if I have no need for intimacy, sensitivity, respect and honesty? There are no objective universal moral absolutes in an atheist world. The humanists who signed the Manifesto might not like my behavior, but ultimately their standards are merely arbitrary and I am not bound to them.

My question to Michael at this point would be,

"Which atheistic approach to ethics will you take?" My contention is that Huxley's is consistent with atheistic presuppositions while the Manifesto's is not. If you subscribe to something like the Manifesto, you need to explain how this is anything other than arbitrary, subjective and conventional. In other words, how can anyone else be seen as being morally obligated to agree with your subjective standards? If your standards are objective and universal, how is this possible in an atheist universe? If you choose something akin to Huxley, are you willing to let Hitler and Stalin practice it? If Hitler was truly morally wrong, tell us how an atheistic worldview can establish his guilt.

And if you concede Huxley's point and admit you have no objective grounds for condemning Hitler, you will still need to explain how an atheist world can account for other laws outside of ethics, such as the laws of logic by which we are debating tonight. And so I want to insist again that atheism cannot even account for this debate. To carry on with the debate is an implicit acknowledgment of Christian Theism. For by appealing to reason, the laws of logic and objective moral standards, we are appealing to standards which make sense in the Christian worldview; yet these standards cannot be accounted for within a universe that is merely matter in motion.

I have heard many atheistic arguments and some of them are quite complex and difficult for me to understand. I freely admit that I came here tonight knowing that my opponent, who is extremely intelligent, might have an argument with which I am unfamiliar or incapable of comprehending without further study. However, whatever argument he uses, it will be something he has devised by the use of reason and logic. Is reason material? I've never seen it, tasted it, smelled it or touched it. If reason is immaterial in nature, how can one account for it in a materialist universe? Once again, I believe that Michael will be depending on the Christian worldview which can make sense of reason, even as he argues against my worldview. If the debate goes poorly for me and I pull out a gun and shoot Michael, would I be guilty of something genuinely immoral, or have I merely acted on my personal brand of situational ethics?

As the late Christian philosopher Dr. Greg Bahnsen argued so persuasively, "The proof of the Christian position is that unless its truth is presupposed, there is no possibility of proving anything at all." Is there a faith commitment on the part of the Christian? Absolutely. But what also ought to be clear, although it is usually left unchallenged, is that the atheist also has faith commitments, and when I compare the two worldviews I am forced to confess that I simply don't have enough faith to be an atheist. Thank you.[124]

---

124   Because this was a transcript, I did not footnote key items. The quotes of Aldous Huxley can be found in his essay, *Ends and Means.* Also see *The Humanist Manifesto II* Paul Kurtz, ed. Prometheus Books, Amherst, New York, 1973.

This was how I presented the Transcendental Argument for God (TAG). My presentation did not delve into the foundations of logic, science and human rights (time was limited), but I did attempt to explore the theistic foundations of objective morality. The *Second Humanist Manifesto* to which I referred in the debate is a very useful prop for contrasting Christian and secular ethical systems. Chapter Eight: "Secular Dreams and Nightmares," made similar use of the *Second Humanist Manifesto* (HMII).

As part of the debate with Michael Allen, there was a brief segment for cross-examination. I used this opportunity to challenge Michael's approach to morality. I had already cited moral judgments he had made on his website, and so I chose to question him about his sense of the foundations of morality. It went as follows:

Jay: Do you think – I would simply like a yes or no at this point – do you believe that Hitler was wrong in his actions?

Michael: Yes.

Jay: Okay, thank you. My second question then would be, why was he wrong?

Michael: Well, again, there are objective frameworks of morality that one can create. For example, it is possible for morality to come about via evolutionary processes. We can see various moral behaviors, for example, in populations of chimpanzees. And the reason it is possible for this to occur, of course, is because morality creates cooperative societies, and it is more efficient to live in a cooperative society than it is to live in a society full of conflict.

Jay: (*I cut in at this point because of time constraints.*) Michael, what if an individual has no desire to be cooperative? Is he not free to choose lack of cooperation?

Michael: Certainly an individual could choose not to be cooperative. However, we are social animals; chimpanzees are social animals. When an individual is not cooperative, when an individual does not cooperate with the group, there are often ramifications from that behavior. And in a cooperative society, which is more efficient than a conflicting society, it increases survival benefits if the individuals can work together.

Jay: If I were a member of the German resistance in 1944, and had been opposed to the larger social cooperative of Nazi Germany, I would be, as an individual, going against the majority. Why would I be wrong?

Michael: Well, I disagree that you would be an individual going against the majority, because, in fact, if you look at the world's reaction to Nazi Germany, the majority was more definitely against Hitler, and there was a world war over that.

Jay: Are you saying, then, that the test for morality is the majority?

Michael: Well, that's part of the test. I mean, there are different sorts of social groups, and there are different kinds of violations of morality that take place. For example, in the Bible in the Ten Commandments you have rules against – do not do this thing, do not do that thing to your neighbor. This is a great example of the in-group morality which was common at the time, and, in fact, if you did something to an outsider in that culture, there was a different standard. So, yes, there are different standards of morality depending on the scope of the social group you are referring to.

Jay: Let's say that over the next twenty years the nature of human opinion changes such that ninety-five percent of all living people believe that the best thing that could happen would be the extermination of the Jews. Would those ninety-five percent be wrong, and, if so, on what basis?

Michael: Well, let's see. Would they be wrong based upon, for example, the extermination of the Amalekites? Certainly, you can't look to the Bible to find that it's wrong to exterminate a particular population, because the example is right there ordered by God. Now what you can do, however, is look at things like empathy, and you could look at things like the increase of human suffering, which must have been very large considering the drowning of the whole world. There was certainly a lot of suffering going on at that time.

Jay: Michael, you have clearly rejected the moral
            basis provided in the Bible, and at this point
            that's not what's being debated. I'm trying to
            explore your basis for morality. If morality
            can somehow be the result of evolution, then
            why can't we say that Hitler's morality was
            the result of how evolution affected him? Why
            would his evolutionary moral code be wrong
            and somebody else's moral code, also the result
            of evolution, be right?

Michael: Again, there's a different standard. I mean,
            history shows us that the overall view of Hitler
            was wrong. There are other standards. We
            can certainly learn from Hitler. We can learn
            about things such as excess nationalism. Here
            again, we go back to an objective standard and
            learn from our mistakes, something we seem
            to have done through slavery, even though
            the Bible condones it. And, so again, we do
            have an objective ability to look at the effects
            of different policies and thoughts on different
            human beings, and we can learn from those
            mistakes and live in a world and create a world
            that is –

Jay: (*I cut in at this point because of time constraints.*)
            In our last few seconds, your understanding
            of the meaning of the word "objective" as it is
            applied to morality is completely irrational.
            How can morality be objective if it is created by
            man?

Michael: Well, it's objective in the sense that we have observations that are looked at and examined and then looked at again by others and compared. You know, the purpose of objectivity in science, for example, is to eliminate the error that comes from subjectivity, and that generally comes from cross-examination of other observations.

Jay: You are equivocating on the meaning of the word objective – that is not what the word means.

(Time expired at this point.)

How I wish I had been permitted more time, but both Michael and I had to operate within the time allotted. Michael's answers to my questions (when he wasn't trying to change the subject) revealed that he wanted to avoid admitting that his basis for moral values was subjective. He is very intelligent and he understood that the Hitler test case would expose the emptiness of subjectivity. His explanation of how we can have objective moral values in an atheist universe was, in my opinion, less than adequate. He claimed:

1) "There are objective frameworks of morality that one can create."

2) "It is possible for morality to come about via evolutionary processes."

3) When asked if the will of the majority is the test for morality, he said, "That's part of the test."

4) When asked how a morality created by man can

be objective, he said, "It's objective in the sense that we have observations that are looked at and examined and then looked at again by others and compared."

Because Michael bears the image of God and has a God-given conscience (Romans 2:14-15), he knew Hitler's policies were immoral. But, regarding Michael's first point, why couldn't Hitler create his own objective framework of morality? Regarding Michael's second point, why couldn't Hitler also appeal to evolution (which is exactly what he did)? Regarding Michael's third point, an appeal to the majority, how does that meet the test of objectivity? Besides, in his next breath, he spoke of "in-group morality" and stated, "There are different standards of morality, depending on the scope of the social group you are referring to." If that is true, then why couldn't the in-group morality of the Nazis be their own standard? If it was "in-group," and each social group can choose its own standard, what difference does it make if those outside the group did not approve? Michael's fourth point, that his moral views are objective because they are based on observation, does not come close to resolving the inconsistencies within his worldview.

The atheist worldview, or at least Michael's version of it, cannot account for objective moral values. Michael sought to use objective moral values to critique Hitler and to critique God. In doing so, Michael was borrowing from the Christian worldview.

Because of the connection between moral standards

and rights, I could have asked Michael about objective human rights. Did the Jews who were murdered in the Nazi death camps possess a universal objective right to life? If they had been stripped of legal rights, did they still possess a right to life that transcends any government or human authority? If so, then how can the existence of a transcendent right be accounted for in an atheist universe? If not, then why do we consider the Nazi's to have been violators of human rights that their victims did not possess?

Appendix B:

The Lucas-Buckner Debate

On March 12, 2010, I had the privilege of publicly debating my friend, Dr. Ed Buckner, who at that time was the President of American Atheists. The debate was part of The Debate Summit 2010, hosted by Grace Community Church of Washington Court House, Ohio. The title of our debate was *Moral Foundations: Which makes more sense, Christianity or Atheism?* On the surface, this was not a debate about the existence of God. Each of us assumed the truth of our own position and then sought to prove that our position gave a better account of human moral concerns than the position of our opponent. Dr. Buckner's worldview presupposed naturalism; God does not exist and there is no supernatural foundation for morality. Because of the close connection between human rights and moral foundations, my debate with Dr. Buckner touched on some of the same ground covered in this book. This Appendix is a transcript of my opening presentation in the debate. At the end of the transcript I will provide a few final comments on the relationship between moral foundations and human rights.

OPENING STATEMENT

Good evening. I want to thank each of you for being here, regardless of where you stand on the issues that Dr. Ed Buckner and I will be debating. And I certainly want to thank Ed for his kindness in our many communications.

There are two basic motives that have brought me here tonight. First of all, I love God and I want His name to be declared and glorified, for this is the highest purpose one can have in life. Secondly, I care about each of you as individuals and I certainly care about Ed. The God who created us can be personally known and to know Him is to know the source of all life and truth.

In keeping with the stated purpose of this debate, I would like to give you a reason for the hope that is within me. It is important to define key terms and to be clear about what we mean by the term "God." The God of Christianity is the eternally self-existent Creator of the universe and He is both transcendent to it and immanent within it. God has made Himself known through the general revelation of the creation, the internal testimony of the human moral conscience, the special revelation of the Scriptures, and, most importantly, through the incarnation of the Son of God, Jesus Christ. The question before us is: **"Moral**

Foundations: Which makes more sense, Christianity or Atheism?" I want to begin my response in defense of Christianity by making a statement that might surprise you. I believe that my friend, Ed Buckner, is not really an atheist but is a theist in rebellion. For as you listen to the debate tonight you will, once you know what to look for, be able to observe not one, but two people who know that God exists. Ed does not want to acknowledge outwardly to others or inwardly to himself something that deep down inside he knows to be true; that there is a just and holy God who has absolute moral standards and that we are accountable to Him. It is Christianity, not atheism that can make sense of moral foundations.

Now, some of you might be thinking that I have just said something terribly offensive by suggesting that Ed is guilty of suppressing what he knows to be true about God. Perhaps this sounds like I am claiming to know Ed better than he knows himself. But let's unpack the claim I have made.

First of all, it is not my claim; what the Bible says in Romans 1:18-21 includes all professing atheists:

> *The wrath of God is being revealed from heaven against all the godlessness and wickedness of men, who suppress the truth by their wickedness, since what may be known about God is plain to them, because God has made it plain to them. For since the creation of the world God's invisible qualities—His eternal power and divine nature—have been clearly seen, being understood from what has*

been made, so that men are without excuse. For although they knew God, they neither glorified Him as God nor gave thanks to Him, but their thinking became futile and their foolish hearts were darkened.[125]

Secondly, please understand that when I apply Romans 1:18-21 to Ed's claim of being an atheist, I speak out of concern and compassion for Ed, as well as for any other atheist who might see or hear this debate. I know that there are several people here tonight who deny that God exists. But since I believe that what the Bible says is true, the most unloving thing I could do would be to leave Ed's professed beliefs unchallenged.

So, where do we go from here? We are here to consider how to make sense of moral foundations. In other words, what is the source or basis for understanding morality and for knowing how to distinguish between right and wrong, and good and evil? By the way, one cannot even acknowledge the real existence of good and evil unless he or she first presupposes the Christian worldview, but we will consider that later. For now, it is very important that we understand what is meant by the words "objective" and "subjective," when we apply them to morality. These terms are the key to our debate tonight.

When we talk about moral standards or foundations as being objective, we are saying that these standards exist outside of or independently from the individual perceiving them. When someone claims morality is subjective, he is

---

125   The New International Version (NIV) was the translation of the Bible used throughout this debate.

saying that morality depends upon the individual. There is no external objective standard which is absolute and universal. Consider this illustration: Two friends are swimming in the ocean which has a temperature of 68 degrees. One swimmer says, "This is too cold," but the other swimmer says, "No, it is just right." Both swimmers have spoken the truth from their own subjective experience. Whether or not it is too cold to swim depends on the individual or subjective view of each swimmer. But the objective truth in this illustration is that the water temperature is 68 degrees. That is objectively true, regardless of the subjective feelings of each swimmer.

To explain how we apply this to moral foundations, let's use a fictional person we will call Jane. One of Jane's moral values is the belief that the rape and torture of children is always wrong. If this value is objective, it means at least this: This value has real existence outside of Jane's personal and individualized value system. It is not just that other people have the same belief as Jane. It is external to them as well. And in the Christian worldview, this value is not just objective, it is universal and absolute. It isn't just wrong for some people to torture and rape a child; it is wrong for everybody at all times and in all places. If we could find someone who took pleasure in the torture and rape of children and he said he sees nothing wrong with it, he would still be in the wrong because there is an objective standard that exists apart from him. Because at least some moral values are objective in nature, their existence does not depend on human beings perceiving them.

What if moral values are only subjective in nature? In Jane's case, this would mean that her opposition to the torture and rape of children is a personal belief that originates within her. It is the result of how her brain works, and this value does not have some kind of objective existence external to people in general and Jane in particular. If moral foundations are subjective, they can still be agreed upon by a community and each value can be rationally debated and decided upon by the group. A whole community of people may agree that they don't want anyone within their community to torture and rape children. The fact that everyone in the community claims to believe that moral foundations are subjective does not mean they cannot reach a consensus as a group. But according to subjectivism, these moral values do not originate outside of the individuals who think of them. Subjective moral values exist only because people create them in their minds.

Do not misunderstand. I am not saying there is no room for subjectivity in morality. But if subjectivity is all we have when it comes to dealing with moral foundations, then there is no ultimate reason not to embrace rape, child molestation, murder or a whole host of behaviors we intrinsically know to be wrong. Unless morality is, at its foundation, objective in nature, there are no real grounds for saying that the child rapist is morally wrong. It might be unpleasant for his victim, but it isn't wrong in any objective, absolute or universal sense. If we want to be logically consistent in saying that the torture and rape of children is always wrong, then we have to presuppose that there exists a universal, absolute moral standard which is objective in nature, and that the rapist is just as bound to it as are the rest of us.

Tonight, you will hear two men argue as though objective moral standards really do exist and that these values stand upon a foundation that enables us to judge not only what is wrong for us to do, but also what is wrong for others as well. Some things are truly and absolutely wrong. But how can we make sense of this in an atheist universe that is nothing more than atoms and molecules in motion, lacking any design or transcendent purpose? An atheist universe cannot provide the pre-conditions necessary for objective, universal and absolute moral values to exist. This leaves us incapable of saying, with logical consistency, that it is always wrong to torture and rape a child for the pleasure of the rapist.

One of the great contemporary philosophers of science, an atheist by the name of Dr. Michael Ruse, has come up with an interesting solution to the atheist dilemma. In his essay entitled *Evolutionary Ethics: A Defense* Dr. Ruse wrote,

> "The evolutionist's case is that ethics is a collective illusion of the human race, fashioned and maintained by natural selection in order to promote individual reproduction ... what is really important to the evolutionist's case is the claim that ethics is illusory in as much as it persuades

us that it has an objective reference. This is
the crux of the biological position."

(page 101)

If it sounds to you as though Dr. Ruse is denying the
existence of objective foundations for ethics and morality,
you are correct. For Ruse, ethics is purely subjective,
the manifestation of human feelings or impulses which
evolution has formed in our brains by chance or accident.
He goes on to say:

> "There are good biological reasons why it is
> part of our nature to objectify morality. If
> we did not regard it as binding, we would
> ignore it. It is precisely because we think
> that morality is more than mere subjective
> desires that we are led to obey it."

(page 102)

Ruse is acknowledging that in a universe without
God, there are no objective grounds for morality.
Fortunately, according to him, evolution has formed our
brains in such a way that we are tricked into believing in
objective morality. Since we have been fooled into believing
this illusion, we live as though common moral standards
are binding, and that keeps most of us from torturing
and raping children. But when a child molester breaks
free of the illusion that there exist objective and binding
moral obligations, where does that leave us? What reason
is there to think that atheism can make sense of moral
foundations? Indeed, I submit that in an atheist universe,

it makes no sense to think of moral foundations as even existing.

I am reminded of the words of famed twentieth century atheist, Dr. Bertrand Russell. In his essay, *A Free Man's Worship*, Russell said:

> "That man is the product of causes that had no prevision of the end thing they were achieving, that his origin, his growth, his hopes and fears, his loves and his beliefs are but the outcome of accidental collocations of atoms, that no fire, no heroism, no intensity of thought and feeling can preserve an individual life beyond the grave. But all the labors of the ages, all the devotion, all the inspirations, all the noon-day brightness of human genius are destined to extinction in the vast death of the solar system, and the whole temple of man's achievements must inevitably be buried beneath the debris of a universe in ruins. All these things, if not quite beyond dispute, are yet so nearly certain that no philosophy which rejects them can hope to stand. Only within the scaffolding of these truths, only on the firm foundation of unyielding despair can the soul's habitation henceforth be safely built.... For man condemned today to lose his dearest, tomorrow himself to pass through the gate of darkness. It remains

only to cherish, ere yet the blow falls, the lofty thoughts that ennoble his little day. Proudly defiant of the irresistible forces that tolerate, for a moment, his knowledge and his condemnation, to sustain alone a weary but unyielding atlas, <u>the world that his own</u> <u>ideals have fashioned</u> despite the trampling march of unconscious power."

That is a poignant description of an atheist universe. According to Russell, man is the product of causes that had no prevision of the end they were achieving and man's beliefs, including our moral beliefs, are nothing more than the outcome of an accidental arrangement of atoms. In such a universe the most consistent way to describe morality is to say it is the product of our own imaginations. What I consider to be moral is the result of the atoms in my brain acting according to the blind physical laws of biochemistry. If the atoms in your brain cause you to choose a different moral standard, neither one of us has objective grounds for judging the other, even if one of us is a rapist.

Remember, the proposition being debated tonight is not the question of whether or not God exists. This particular debate allows Ed and me each to assume a worldview and then use it to make sense of moral foundations. We have seen that if we assume atheism and are honest about its implications, we are reduced to acknowledging that ultimately ethics is an illusion, and the moral beliefs of those who oppose the torture and rape of a child are not superior to the moral beliefs of the rapist. Different? Yes. Superior? No.

Before concluding my opening presentation, I want to state very clearly that I believe Ed Buckner is a morally sensitive man who would unreservedly condemn the child rapist. And I agree that in one sense, people can be good without acknowledging God. But I would like to speak as a friend when I say to Ed that if we accept an atheist universe, all the reasons Ed might offer for justifying his condemnation of rape are arbitrary in nature.

I find it interesting that Ed belongs to the Council for Secular Humanism, which in 1980 published a Declaration which spells out the central beliefs and claims of Secular Humanism. On the question of morality the Declaration says, "Morality that is not God-based need not be anti-social, subjective, or promiscuous, nor need it lead to the breakdown of moral standards." Notice the attempt to distance itself from subjectivity. A few sentences later the Declaration says, "We are opposed to absolutist morality, yet we maintain that objective standards emerge, and ethical values and principles may be discovered, in the course of ethical deliberation." This Declaration at least seems to recognize the need for objective standards. I remind you, however, of the earlier citation of the atheist biologist Dr. Michael Ruse, who said, "The evolutionist's case is the claim that ethics is illusory in as much as it persuades us that it has an objective reference."

Although Ed is affiliated with the group which issued the Declaration, he apparently is closer to Dr. Ruse's position. In April of 2002, Ed debated Rev. John Rankin, covering some of the same ground we are addressing tonight. In that debate, Ed denied objectivity and went so far as to claim that even the very definition or standard of goodness is purely subjective. His exact words were, "Subjective definitions of good are all we have."

If Ed argues here tonight as he has on other occasions, then you will hear him criticize God and the Bible for all sorts of evil and suffering. You might hear him claim things such as the Bible supports human slavery and the mistreatment of women or that God is unjust in His judgments against violations of His commands or that the prevalence of human suffering is proof that God does not exist. It is a matter of public record that Ed thinks the Christian God is very immoral.

If Ed makes these arguments, he will be smuggling in an unspoken premise that he outwardly denies. Ed will be acting as though there are objective moral absolutes and objective definitions of good that he can use to judge God, and to find God guilty. The fact that he might be twisting Scripture or taking it out of context is secondary to the fact that he believes he is privy to a standard of goodness and morality that allows him to judge other people or even God Himself. And the moment he does that, you will have first-hand evidence that Ed is not really an atheist, but a theist in rebellion. For in an atheist universe, there can be no timeless and unchanging moral foundations or standards by which a person can be ethically bound and judged by others. An atheist universe cannot make sense of the standards Ed will be using. As atheist Bertrand Russell said, "Man's beliefs are the outcome of accidental arrangements of atoms that had no prevision of the ends they were achieving." In such a universe, everything about man, including his ethics, is the result of a series of accidents.

Every time you hear Ed criticize God, the Bible or Christians, remind yourself to ask Ed the big question, "Why?" Why are Ed's moral sensitivities and standards of goodness, which he admits are totally subjective, binding on anyone? What gives him the right to judge someone who has chosen different standards than his? His worldview cannot make sense of moral foundations.

On the other hand, Christianity can make perfect sense of Ed's moral sensitivities and of yours and mine, too. Although claiming to be an atheist, Ed cannot escape the way God has made him. Ed has a God-given moral conscience with which he must contend. In Romans 2:14-15, the Apostle Paul explained how it is that even people who have never read the written law of God share common moral values:

> *Indeed, when Gentiles, who do not have the law, do by nature things required by the law, they are a law for themselves, even though they do not have the law, since they show that the requirements of the law are written on their hearts, their consciences also bearing witness, and their thoughts now accusing, now even defending them.*

I invite all of you in the audience tonight to ask yourself whether you believe there are some actions so immoral that they are wrong at all times, for all cultures and in all conditions? If so, ask yourself which worldview makes better sense of that phenomenon, an atheist universe that exists by accident without design or ultimate purpose, or the Christian worldview that says humanity bears the image of God and that we share a moral conscience given to us by the God who created us? On the other hand, if you deny that objective universal moral absolutes exist and if you claim that there is no such thing as a God-given moral conscience, why should your individual subjective standards be binding on anyone else? When carefully considered, I believe it is Christianity, not atheism, that can make sense of moral foundations.

(End of opening presentation)

The argument I made against Ed's subjective foundation for morality can just as easily be made against a subjective foundation for human rights. The lack of an objective, universal and unchanging standard for rights reduces human rights to the personal preferences of whoever has enough power to make the rules. Suppose a young woman in China is pregnant with her second child and the Chinese government informs her that she must have an abortion as part of China's population control policies. Is there a universal human right to life possessed by the mother and the baby that supersedes a government-ordered abortion? Not in an atheist universe.

Suppose a mother already had two children, aged five and six, and a new law was passed which said one of the children must be eliminated in order to reduce the population. Is this a genuine human rights violation? Not in an atheist universe. I have no doubts that many atheists would join ranks with Christians in order to oppose that law, but they would have no basis for appealing to a universal human right to life. They would have to borrow capital from the Christian worldview to make such an appeal.

Appendix C:

An Open Letter To Non-Christians

Dear Non-Christian Reader,

Greetings. I want to thank you for having read far enough to get to this letter, unless of course you have skipped everything except this letter! If you finish this and then read the rest of this book, there is a good probability you will be offended. Please understand that I have no desire to offend or anger you, but given the nature of the topic at hand and the atmosphere of our postmodern culture, some of what I say might bother you. Please don't let that stop you from finishing.

I would like to lay my cards out on the table and let you see my hand. I will not try to justify my beliefs to you here. The book which contains this letter explains the reason for the hope that is within me. The God we encounter in the Bible, beginning in Genesis 1, does exist.

Many of the particular beliefs I am about to share with you are not defended in this book, but that primary assertion, that God exists, has been defended. My prayer for you is that you will come to know Him in a manner consistent with what the Bible teaches.

Are you ready? Here it is: There is a God. Not just any god, but the God we read about in the Bible. He is eternal, He is all-knowing and all-powerful, and He is good. He created all things, and the life you now possess is due to Him. You are accountable to God and will someday appear before Him to render that account. Here's where things get problematic. Like me, you are a sinner. This means that you have violated, both by commission and omission, the standards of God. We are criminals in God's universe. God is righteous and in His holy nature, He cannot ignore your sin. The guilt of sin will be punished in a manner reflecting God's perfect justice. If God were to leave sin unpunished, He would be untrue to His own character. We are capable of such inconsistencies; He is not.

Is there a remedy for the problem of sin? Well, many have been suggested, and all but one are wrong. The three most common errors are denial, blame shifting, and religion. Denial is the answer of the atheist and the agnostic: If I can convince myself there is no God, then there is no problem. No God, no sin, no accountability. Those who choose this path are self-deceived, and deep down they know they are wrong, but they refuse to acknowledge it.

The second erroneous remedy is blame-shifting.

In this scenario, I don't deny my sin, just my personal responsibility for it. There are several options available under this umbrella. I can blame others (parents, spouse, society). I can blame physiology (my doctor told me it's not my fault and he's up on the latest science). I can even blame God for how He has made me or for the circumstances in which He has placed me.

Finally, I can try to provide my own remedy for sin through being religious. Yes, I have done some wrong things, but I can compensate for them or negate them by the good things I do on the other side of the ledger. I am basically a good person and I certainly haven't done some of the bad things I have seen others do. After all, it's not like I'm a mass murderer! On balance, I think when God looks at my overall record and the religious things I do, He will accept me.

I recognize that the vast majority of people think of themselves as being basically good. But consider the Ten Commandments (Exodus 20:1-17), for example: "Thou shall not steal." Have you ever stolen anything, no matter how small? If so, you are a thief. Have you ever knowingly deceived someone? If so, you are a liar. Have you ever had hateful thoughts toward someone? According to Jesus, that makes you a murderer (Matthew 5:21-22). Have you ever looked at someone and had lustful thoughts? If so, that makes you an adulterer (Matthew 5:27-28). And those are just four of the commandments. Care to look at the other six?

Humanly speaking, there was a reason Jesus was crucified. He upset too many people by saying things they found to be offensive or threatening to the status quo. I have no doubt that if Jesus were living in America today, He would not be very popular. Although He would love atheists, He would rebuke them for being foolish (in the biblical sense of the word; Psalm 14:1). Although He would be compassionate, He would not allow the blame-shifters to hide behind their excuses. Instead, He would call upon them to repent. Jesus would be especially emphatic with those who believe their religious deeds make them righteous in God's eyes. He would tell them the standard for satisfying God's righteousness is perfection. Unless they are perfect (and Jesus would point out the ways in which they are not perfect), all of their religiosity is an exercise in empty self-righteousness.

Those unpopular teachings were some of the human reasons Jesus was crucified. But God had His own reasons for sending His Son to die, and He was proactive in the process. If you want to have your mind stretched, consider these words which Peter spoke in Jerusalem less than two months after Jesus was crucified:

> *"Men of Israel, hear these words: Jesus of Nazareth, a man attested to you by God with mighty works and wonders and signs that God did through Him in your midst, as you yourselves know – this Jesus, delivered up according to the definite plan and foreknowledge of God, you crucified and killed by the hands of lawless men."*

Acts 2:22-23

According to Scripture, Jesus' death atoned for sins. He was sinless; I was the guilty one. God decreed that Jesus would pay my penalty for me. He bore the righteous wrath of God that my sins deserved. How much of my own merit, goodness or service will God count towards my forgiveness and justification? Zero, none, nada, nothing. It is by His grace alone, through faith alone, in Jesus Christ alone. God showed His acceptance and approval of Jesus' sacrificial death by raising Him from the dead. I thank God for the empty tomb. You will receive forgiveness for your sins, the gift of eternal life, and the RIGHT to be a child of God, if you repent of your sins and entrust yourself by faith, into the person and sacrifice of Jesus Christ.

Well, now that just about everyone under the sun is offended, let's add the final straw. Heaven is a possibility, but there is only one way to get there. It is through Jesus Christ. Yes, in a day which exalts pluralism and tolerance, the message of biblical Christianity fails to change with the times. Come to think of it, there is one additional claim. If you reject the gospel of Jesus Christ, the consequence of that rejection is eternal damnation in Hell.

Outraged? Amused? Offended? Before you use this book to light a campfire or line a birdcage, let's consider something. Let's say, just for the sake of argument, that you believed and personally accepted the truth in the claims about which you just read. What would the rest of us have to conclude about you if we knew you believed those things, yet YOU SAID NOTHING? How could you believe it was possible to have one's sins forgiven, and then keep that knowledge to yourself?...that someone could receive eternal life as a gift...that someone could be given the right to become a child of God ...that God could be known in a personal, fulfilling and liberating way...that Hell is a real place and many are on the path of destruction that leads to it, but by believing the good news of Jesus Christ they could be saved...that it is possible to be adopted into God's family and become a co-heir with Jesus Christ...how could you believe all these things and then not proclaim them and invite others to embrace them? I know this: We would have grounds for questioning your love and compassion. To possess such information yet keep it to yourself is unconscionable. So what if some people would be critical of you and perhaps resent you for your beliefs? You might be ridiculed. But if you had even an ounce of compassion for people and if you took scriptural commands seriously, you would speak up.

I have written *The Rights Fight* for several reasons. The main reason is that I love God and delight in proclaiming Him to others. As a pastor and as the director of The Isaac Backus Project, I care about the spiritual welfare of fellow Christians and want them to be confident that what the Bible says about God is true. But I also count it a privilege to interact with people who are not Christians. Yes, I desire to see them converted to Christianity. I desire that for you.

Nowadays, non-Christians are often offended when Christians testify about their faith in Jesus Christ and seek to persuade others of their need for Him. In light of what I just said, I wonder if it might not be more appropriate for non-Christians to be offended by Christians who DON'T share their faith. I leave that to you to decide.

Finally, let me confess to something that might seem completely contradictory. I don't believe that very many people are converted to Christianity through rational arguments such as those found in *The Rights Fight*. [126] That's quite an admission, considering the huge time commitment required to write this book. I can tell you in complete honesty, however, that if only a single person comes to faith in Jesus Christ through this book and the hundreds of additional books and articles written by others, that one soul is worth the time and effort. Perhaps that person will be you.

But as precious as one soul is, rational argument is always important, even if no one responds. Christianity calls us to exercise faith, but it is not a blind faith and it is not irrational. The universe we live in was created by a God who is the very source of truth. He calls us to know the truth, believe the truth and submit to the truth. He *is* the Truth. I find endless joy in seeing how God's truth is manifested in many various and wonderful ways. One of the ways God makes His truth known is through the existence of the conscience ingrained in each of us. Our God-given consciences testify to us about the existence of human rights. The rational presentation of that truth is the basis of *The Rights Fight*. I thank God for the privilege of writing it and sharing it with you.

Grace to you.

---

126   This resistance is not because Christianity is irrational. As has been argued elsewhere, the very existence of rationality depends on the truthfulness of the Christian worldview. I believe what G.K. Chesterton said is true:, "The Christian ideal has not been tried and found wanting; it has been found difficult and left untried."

About The Author

Jay Lucas is the Director of The Isaac Backus Project, a ministry dedicated to training Christians in apologetics and equipping them to engage the culture with Biblical truth. He also serves as the Senior Pastor of Grace Community Church in Washington Court House, Ohio.

Jay has pastored churches in New York and Ohio and has served as an adjunct instructor at Baptist Bible College (PA), Cedarville University (OH) and The Cornerstone Seminary (CA). He also serves on the Advisory Board for Cedarville University's Center for Bioethics and is both a member of the Board of Directors and a speaker for Creation Training Initiative.

Jay and his wife, Becky, have six children. They reside in New Holland, Ohio.

For more information,
visit www.theisaacbackusproject.com

Need additional copies?

To order more copies of
The Rights Fight,
contact NewBookPublishing.com

❐ Order online at NewBookPublishing.com

❐ Call 877-311-5100 or

❐ Email Info@NewBookPublishing.com

Call for multiple copy discounts!

Reliance
Media